P9-ECT-298

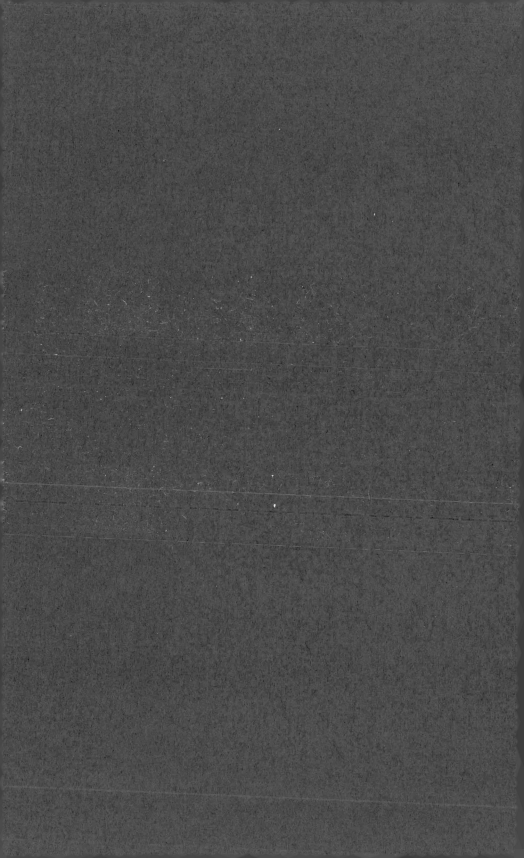

SHOGI
Japan's Game of Strategy

歩
P

香
L

桂
Kt

銀
S

金
G

角
B

飛
R

王
K

SHOGI

Japan's Game of Strategy

by TREVOR LEGGETT

CHARLES E. TUTTLE COMPANY

Rutland, Vermont & Tokyo, Japan

Representatives

For Continental Europe:
BOXERBOOKS, INC., Zurich

For the British Isles:
PRENTICE-HALL INTERNATIONAL, INC., London

For Australasia:
PAUL FLESCH & CO., PTY. LTD., Melbourne

For Canada:
M. G. HURTIG LTD., Edmonton

Published by the Charles E. Tuttle Company, Inc.
of Rutland, Vermont & Tokyo, Japan
with editorial offices at
Suido 1-chome, 2-6, Bunkyo-ku, Tokyo, Japan

Library of Congress Catalog Card No. 66-11011

International Standard Book No. 0-8048-0526-1

First edition, 1966
Third printing, 1973

Book design & typography by Keiko Chiba

PRINTED IN JAPAN

If you wish to purchase a Shogi set, please write a note or postcard directly to the Charles E. Tuttle Co., Inc., Rutland, Vermont, U.S.A.

TABLE OF CONTENTS

INTRODUCTION

SHOGI is the Japanese representative of the family of chess games, offshoots of the Indian *chatur-anga* which was traditionally invented by the legendary Emperor Ravana to exercise his generals in strategy and tactics. *Chatur-anga* literally means four limbs, and some authorities believe it referred to the four "arms" of the military in India: elephants, chariots (or boats), horses, and foot.

The name became corrupted to *shatranj* when it spread westward to Persia, which introduced it to Europe. The chess words "check" and "mate" are from the Persian *shah* (king) and *mat* (dead). The traditional elephant remains symbolized by the castle, or Rook, because originally the archers shot from a howdah on the back of the elephant. The horse has become a Knight, with the same peculiar move in the Far West and Far East. The foot soldiers are Pawns the world over, usually with the right to advance only in single steps. Their power to capture, however, varies in the different forms of chess.

The object of the game is everywhere the same—to capture the leader of the opposing forces, generally by depriving him of most of his men first. In the West this leader is the King, but to the Chinese a second Emperor on a level with the first was inconceivable, and the Chinese game is fought out between two "commanders-in-chief."

In the course of time the Chinese made considerable alterations. Instead of the castling maneuver, the commander is provided with a special enclosure which he cannot leave; he has a special bodyguard of two retainers who remain in it with him. An early allusion to the game is supposed to date from about 570 A.D. The Chinese later incorporated an entirely new piece which is like a Rook except that it must jump over another piece and can then capture anything on the line beyond. This piece is called a Cannon, and a twelfth-century text mentions a mock war game in which each side has sixteen men: two Cannons, two Elephants, two Horses, two Chariots, two Knights, one Commander, and five Foot.

The game went to Korea and is believed to have entered Japan in different forms about the eighth century. However there is considerable confusion and few reliable records. When it first came to Japan the board was probably already nine squares each way, the pieces totaling 36. The elephants had become Gold and Silver generals.

It is thought that Shogi had already divided into two or even more forms by the time it reached Japan. The simplest was begun with the pieces on the back rank, or horizontal row of squares, with the Pawns on the second rank—rather like the Western chess opening position. The game must have been extremely tame because most of the pieces could only move one square at a time. The Japanese courtiers soon livened up the play by introducing (or rather re-introducing) the Rook, the Bishop, and some fresh pieces. At one time no less than six Japanese forms of the game were current:

Little Shogi, in which one Elephant was restored, and two Leopards, a Flying Chariot (Rook), and a Diagonal Runner (Bishop) were added, making 46 pieces in all;

Middle Shogi, with a board of 12 squares each way and 92 pieces;

Great Shogi, with a board of 15 squares each way and 130 pieces;

Great-Great Shogi, 17 squares each way and 192 pieces;

Maka-Great-Great Shogi, 19 squares each way and 192 pieces. (*Maka* is the Japanese rendering of Sanskrit *Maha,* meaning great, so the game is called Great^3 Shogi);

Tai-Shogi, a final supreme chess-to-end-all-chess, invented by some recreational megalomaniac with a board 25 squares each way and a total of 354 pieces.

The opening set-up of a game of Maka-Great-Great Shogi is like a menagerie. The first rank is presumably human, with its Gold, Silver, Copper, Iron, Stone, and Clay generals, but the next four ranks are a jungle of Furious Dragons, Raging Tigers, Blind Boars, Soaring Phoenixes, Hard-Biting Wolves, Thrashing Serpents, and even the odd Cat and Old Rat. In front of this horde is a single line of 19 stolid Pawns. In the rear is the Commander who might well say like the Duke of Wellington at a march-past, "I don't know what effect they'll have on the enemy, but by Heaven they frighten me!"

One would think that the play must have been hopelessly confused; however, we know that this mastodon of a game was actually played. On September 12, 1142 a minister at court recorded in his diary that he played Maka-Great-Great Shogi in the Imperial presence, adding the pathetic note, "I lost."

Towards the end of the sixteenth century a great purge was made, and the game was standardized to a board 9 squares each way and a total of 40 pieces. The reform is traditionally attributed to the Emperor Go-Nara who based it on Little Shogi minus the Elephants and Leopards. This talented Emperor is also supposed to have introduced the revolutionary rule by which a captured piece becomes the property of the capturing side and can be dropped on the board. The rule is the special characteristic of Japanese chess, found in no other game of the family. It gives Shogi a peculiar excitement, which was doubtless necessary to replace the lost thrills of lions and tigers.

Shogi was taken up by three great generals of sixteenth-seventeenth-century Japan: Nobunaga, Hideyoshi, and Ieyasu. They esteemed it for its original purpose, namely as an exercise in military strategy and tactics. Ieyasu became sole ruler of Japan, and under his patronage the game was popular with high and low.

In the seventeenth century the first championships were held. The second champion, Ohashi, established the rules, including a new rule against the repetition of moves. The championship descended, in the Japanese fashion, in the Ohashi and Ito families. (This does not work out so badly as might be expected because of the Japanese custom of adopting into the family the favorite pupil, to whom certain trade secrets are then imparted.) Early in the twentieth century the granting of the title was formally surrendered to the All-Japan Shogi Association, to be competed for regularly.

At present Shogi players are organized in two classes, professionals and amateurs. There is a ranking system under which a beginner enters in the 15th *kyu* class and works his way down until he becomes 1st *kyu*. This is a reasonable amateur level. The next step is to 1st *dan* grade, and then he goes up through the *dans*. In the 8th *dan* there are generally some 30–40 masters, with probably fewer in the 7th and

6th *dan* ranks below. Three living masters have attained 9th *dan* rank (which is fought out among the 8th *dans*), and they are all also championship holders.

Amateurs do well if they get a 1st *dan* grade certificate from the All-Japan Shogi Association; the top rank ever held by an amateur is 5th *dan*.

Shogi is extremely popular among all classes. There is almost no magazine without a column on it, and the evening editions of the big daily papers feature some current tournament game, giving a few moves and a long commentary. A top Shogi master thus can make a reasonably good living by writing articles and books for the very wide Shogi public and by giving lessons. Some of the masters are striking personalities in their own right and well-known figures on the Japanese scene. For instance former champion Yoshio Kimura, when he retired from tournament play, overnight became a television star noted for his sharp wit.

SHOGI

Japan's Game of Strategy

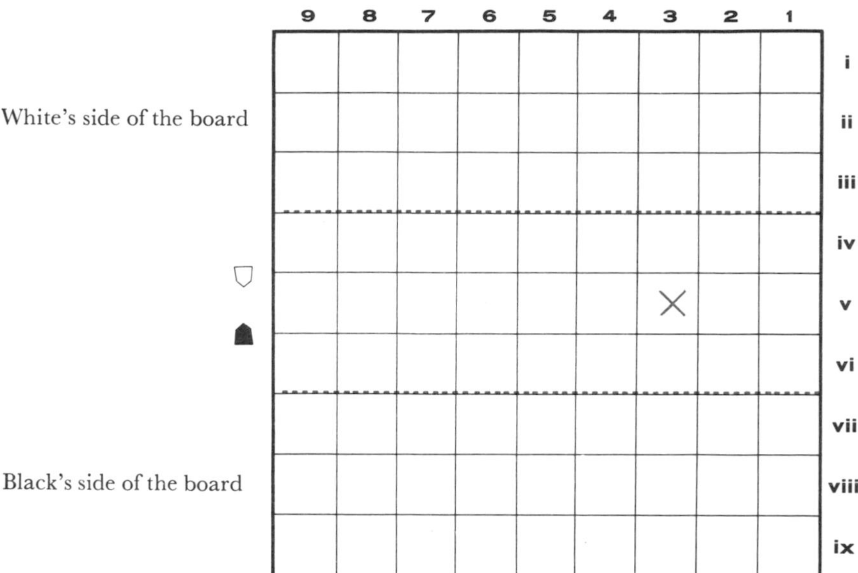

THE BOARD AND THE MEN

I. The Board

THE BOARD is 9 squares each way, giving 81 squares in all. In fact it's not quite square but oblong, and you play down the length of it. There are no colors, either on the board or the pieces. The pieces are only distinguished by the way they point. Black is on the side nearest to us, and White opposite. The first move is Black's.

The squares are identified, as you see, by two co-ordinates, Roman numbers one way and Arabic numbers the other. The Arabic numbers are read first, so that if we say "King–3 v," it would mean that the King (wherever he is) moves to the third column's fifth square, or the spot marked X on the diagram. (The Japanese books use the same numbers across the top but use the Japanese numbers down. In the Appendix we shall explain how you can easily learn these so that you can read a real Japanese score.)

The two dotted lines are the "promotion lines" which are imagined to run across the board, and to help us keep them in mind, they are marked with a couple of thick black dots on the actual board. When your pieces get to the other side of the far promotion line, or when his pieces get to your side of the near promotion line, those pieces are "promoted," that is, they change their powers if desired. Details will be explained later.

Notice we have incorporated the main character, which will help you recognize him easily when you move on to the Japanese Shogi books.

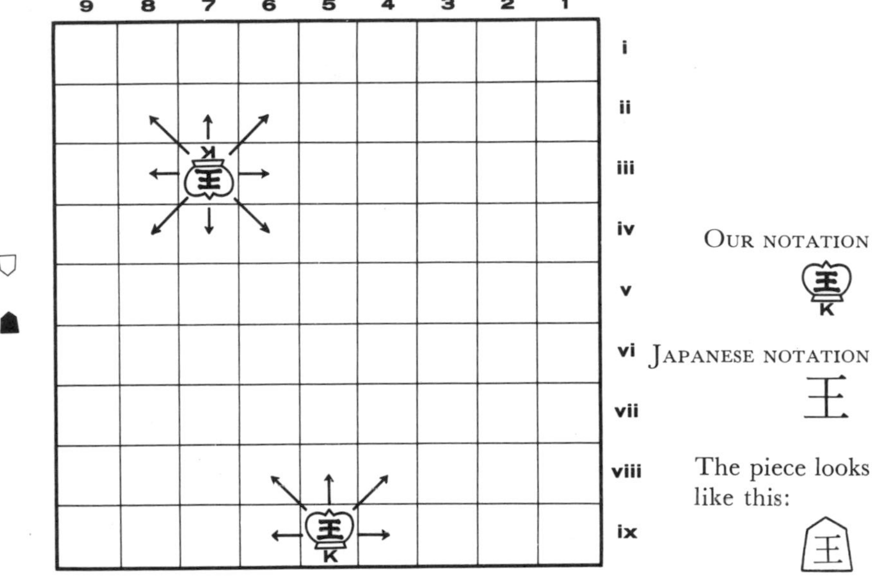

II. The King

The King is like our chess King, short-sighted and cautious. He can travel just one square with each move. He starts in the middle; Black's King (the one nearest to us) is on his original square. His possible moves are as shown. White's King (the one further away) started on 5 i, but he has made two moves, first to 6 ii and then to 7 iii. From there he can go to any square which touches his, as shown in the diagram.

The King is the quarry; the game is to capture (checkmate) him, as in chess. In the Japanese game he nearly always stays in one of the corners and has to have quite a royal guard round him to deal with "paratroops," which are a special feature of Shogi.

You notice that there's no difference of color between the Kings (though they are called "Black" and "White"). In Shogi all the pieces are distinguished by the way they are facing. White's King, looking upside down just as he does on the board, is the enemy because he is pointing towards us. So with all the other pieces.

Like all Shogi pieces, the King when he moves can:

(1) go to any vacant square, or

(2) move onto a square where there is an *enemy* piece.

In the latter case, the enemy piece is removed from the board and becomes the property of the capturing side.

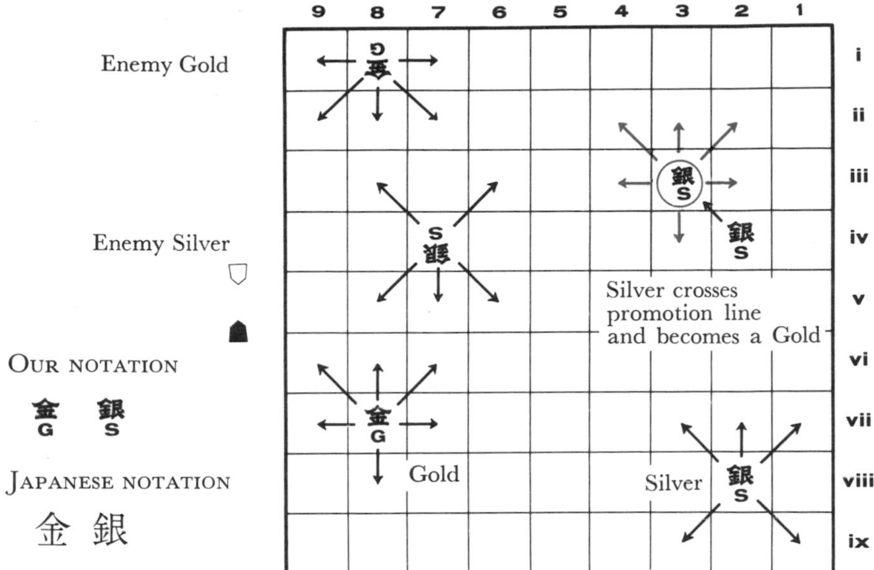

III. The King's Bodyguard: Gold and Silver

The Gold's full name is Gold General. He's really a slightly weaker King in power, and one of his main functions is to stay beside his King to defend him.

He can go to any square touching his present square, *except* the two diagonal rear squares. His possible moves are shown on the left of the diagram. He has the three frontal squares, the ones straight to each side, and the one straight back.

The Gold is never promoted; he stays himself wherever he is. Most of the other pieces, when promoted, turn into Golds.

The Silver, too, is a sort of weaker King. He has the three frontal squares just like the Gold, but in retreat all he is allowed is the two diagonal rear squares. He can't go straight back or straight to the side. Somehow you must make yourself associate the curly "S" with the diagonal rear directions. This will stop your confusing him with the Gold.

When a Silver makes all or part of his move beyond the promotion line on the far side, you *may,* on that move, promote him to Gold. This means that he gains slightly more power but he also *loses* his power of diagonal retreat, so quite often it pays you to forego the privilege for a move or two. A Silver, or any other piece whose promotion is optional, must be promoted on a move *prior* to the one in which it uses its promoted powers.

To show a promoted Silver in our diagrams, we put a ring around him; remember this means that he moves as a Gold. We don't write him as a Gold because it is important to know that he was originally Silver. On the actual Shogi pieces the promotion is indicated on the reverse side.

More About Gold and Silver

Like most of the Shogi pieces, the Gold is poor in retreating, and this means that he must not be pushed forward too soon. The two Golds nearly always stay in their own lines to defend the King, and sometimes to prevent a break-through on the Rook's side as well. The Golds have their initial position on either side of the King, and they try to go with him when he fortifies himself in one corner or the other. Think of the Gold as a *defensive* piece; he doesn't go out to attack, as a rule.

The Silver on the other hand has two retreating squares, namely the two diagonals. These diagonal moves are very handy for threading his way in between the Pawns. The Silver is partly defensive, but also partly attacking. Generally one Silver stays at home (with his two Gold colleagues) to protect the King, but the other Silver goes out and tries to penetrate into the enemy lines, in co-operation with the Rook, Bishop, and maybe a Knight (which comes into action last of all). Whereas the Gold is a heavy-weight, the Silver is of lighter metal, alternately attacking and retreating to break up the opponent's formation with feints and threats.

Several openings are named after Silver, depending on how the attacking Silver is used. There is no opening named after the Gold, and this gives you the hint that the Golds usually stay at home.

He corresponds exactly to the Rook in our chess; so we have simply put the Japanese character inside our own castle.

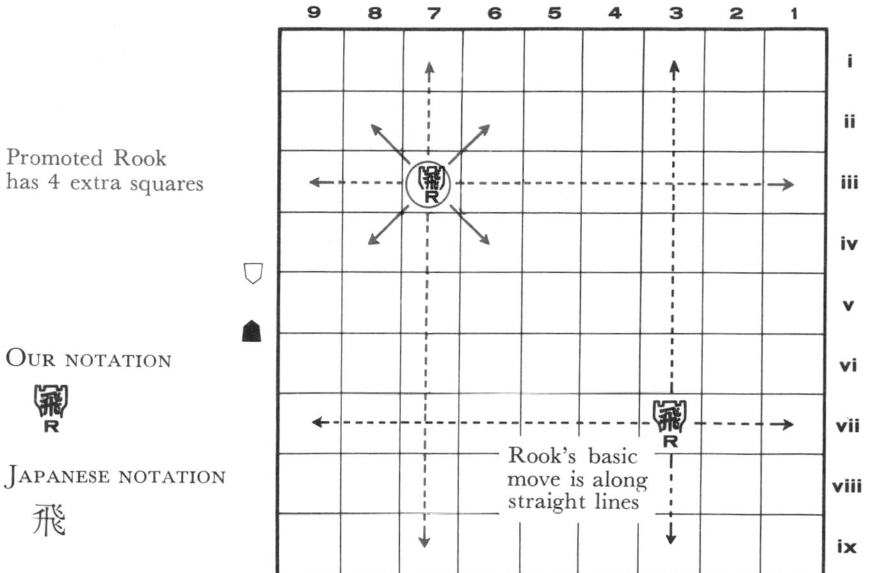

IV. The Rook

The Rook moves any number of squares along a rank or file, horizontally or vertically. If he comes to an enemy piece, he can take it and place himself on that same square. If he comes to a piece from his own side, he must stop short. He cannot jump.

The Rook on the right in the diagram is at 3 vii. He can move anywhere along file 3 or anywhere along rank vii until he comes to another piece if there is one, as explained above.

When the Rook passes the promotion line on the far side of the board, or when he makes his whole move inside enemy territory on the far side of that line, he may be promoted. This means that he can move an extra *one square along any of the diagonals,* in addition to keeping his original powers as a Rook. The Rook on the top left has been promoted, and his extra squares are as marked. Note that he only gets the one extra square on any diagonal; he's not a full chess Queen.

When the Rook gets promoted, we put a ring around him in the diagram to show it.

He's just like our Bishop, so we have put the Japanese characters inside our own Bishop emblem.

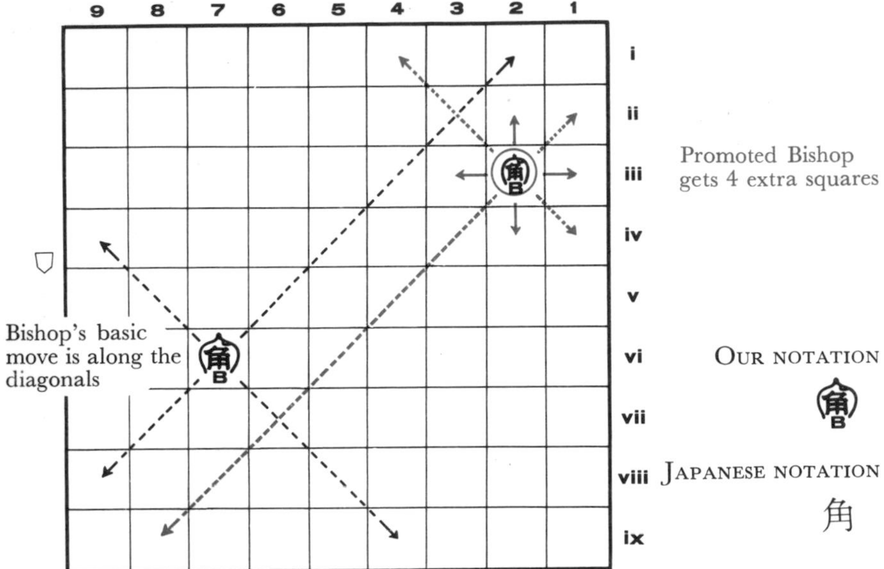

V. The Bishop

The Bishop, like the chess Bishop, runs along the diagonal lines to any square he likes, until he meets a piece if there is one. If that piece is an enemy piece, he can take it and put himself on the same square; if the piece is one of his own, he must stop at the square short of it or some previous square.

Like the Rook, he gets his special promotion when he crosses, or makes his whole move beyond, the distant promotion line. His extra power is *one square along any of the straight lines* (ranks or files). He keeps his basic power.

The Bishop and Rook are the big guns of the Shogi board, but each side has only one of them to start out with. The openings all depend on freeing lines for their operation. Because the Japanese board is bigger (and has no colors), you have to watch the Bishop's diagonals carefully.

As a rule the Bishop gets going much earlier than the Rook, though when the latter does lumber into action, he does great execution. Normally the Rook is worth a bit more than the Bishop, though there are quite a lot of positions (particularly in the opening) where it will pay to capture his Bishop at the cost of your Rook. At a rough valuation, both Rook and Bishop are each worth a bit more than two Golds, or than Gold and Silver.

He strongly resembles the chess Knight, so we have put the Japanese character inside the conventional horse-head:

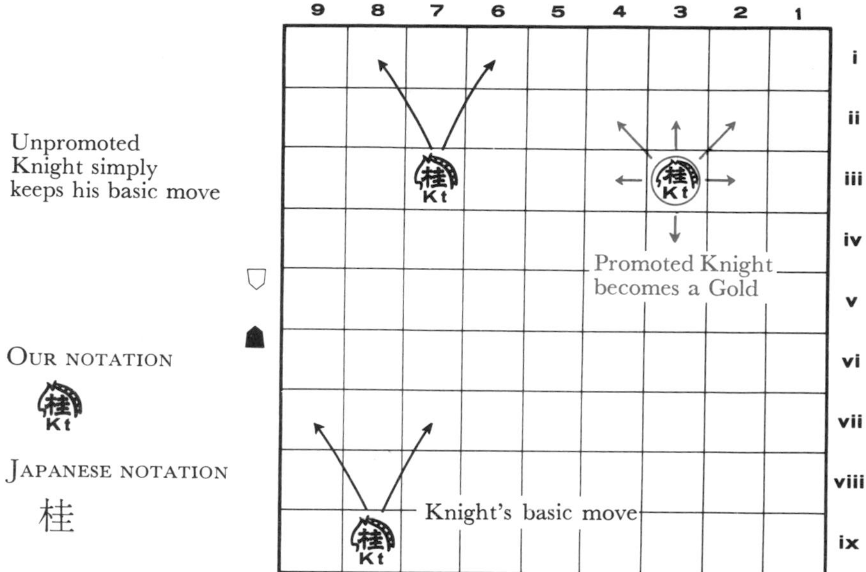

VI. The Knight

The Shogi Knight has the same curious move as the chess Knight, but he can only make it to the front. So the Shogi Knight's move is *one square straight forward, and then one to either diagonal to the front.* He cannot go to the side, nor can he retreat.

As in chess, he is a *jumper,* the only piece that cannot be blocked on his path. He can land on a free square or a square on which there is an enemy piece (which he takes as he lands). But he cannot land on a square already occupied by one of his own men.

When he crosses the far promotion line, you *may* promote him to a Gold, or you can leave him as he is. But if he reaches the last two ranks, you *must* promote him, as otherwise he would have no further move.

The Knight does not begin to move early in the opening because he cannot retreat, and if he comes out too soon he gets attacked. Then all he can do is go on deeper and deeper among the enemy men, who make way for him and then close in. The Knights should come out in the early middle game, when all the other pieces are placed just as you need them.

This is a new piece.

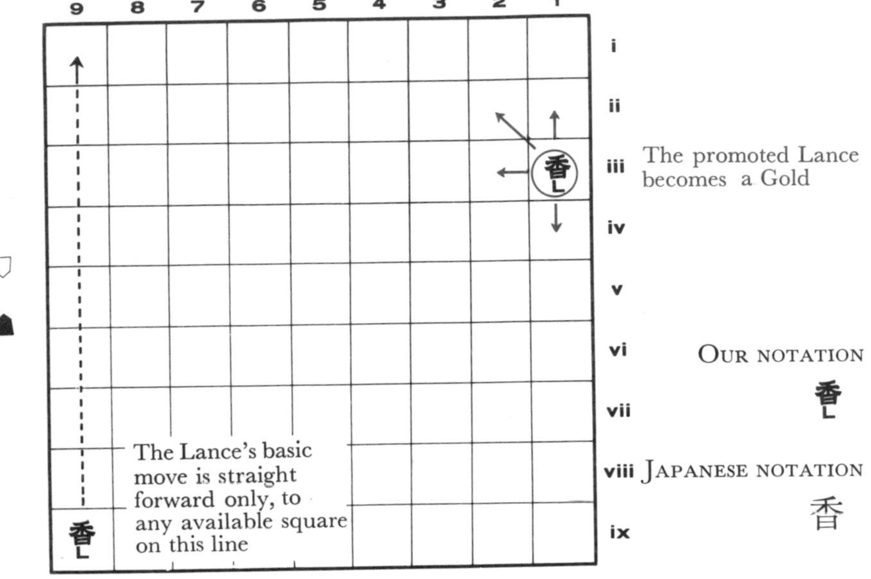

VII. The Lance

The Lance is a new piece, but a very simple one. He is like a Rook, but he can only travel *straight forward,* never to the side and never backwards.

When he crosses the distant promotion line, or makes his whole move beyond it, he *may* be promoted into a Gold. But if he reaches the last rank, he *must* be promoted into a Gold, as otherwise he would have no move. When promoted to Gold, he loses his original powers, and occasionally it pays not to promote him.

The Lance's starting position is at the edge of the board, where we show him on the left, so he does not have much say in things until the opposing King has castled, or rather fortified himself in that corner. Then the Lance comes into his own. Like the Knight in Shogi, the Lance is a late starter. If you try to bring him out too soon, you just lose him because he cannot retreat.

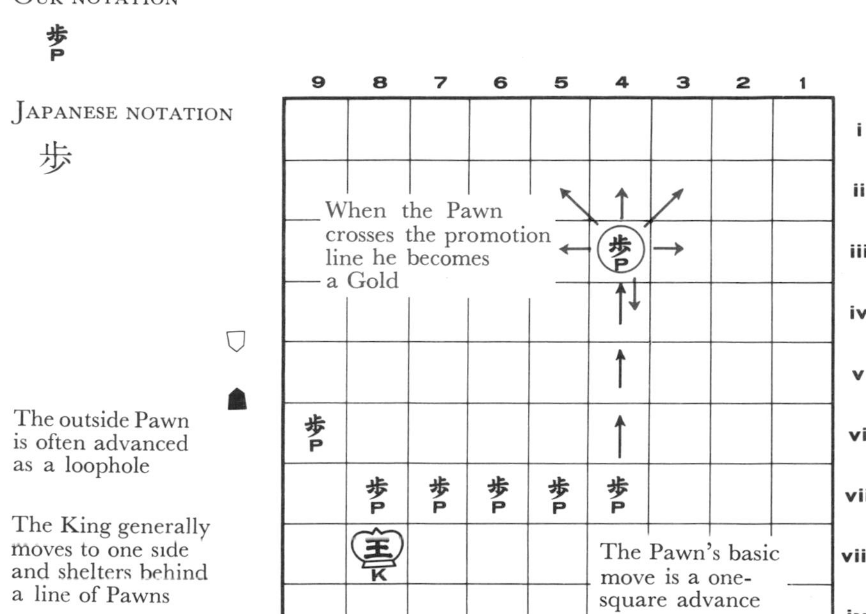
OUR NOTATION
歩
P
JAPANESE NOTATION
歩
9 8 7 6 5 4 3 2 1
i
ii
iii
iv
v
vi
vii
viii
ix
When the Pawn crosses the promotion line he becomes a Gold
The outside Pawn is often advanced as a loophole
The King generally moves to one side and shelters behind a line of Pawns
The Pawn's basic move is a one-square advance
王
K

VIII. The Pawn

The Pawn is the same one-square man as in chess, but here he is also a one-track man. He moves *forward one square at a time* (without the option of a jump on the first move), and he captures in the same way (i.e. the piece on the square in front of him). Therefore the Pawn cannot be blockaded by an enemy piece—he just takes it. He only gets blocked by his own men. Like the chess Pawn, he can *never retreat.*

When the Pawn crosses the far promotion line, he is always promoted to a Gold.

Pawns start out in line on the third rank. As in chess, it does not pay to advance too many of them at the beginning. You need to keep three back for your King to shelter behind, and also as in chess, there is a safety precaution of moving one Pawn a square forward to give the King a bolthole.

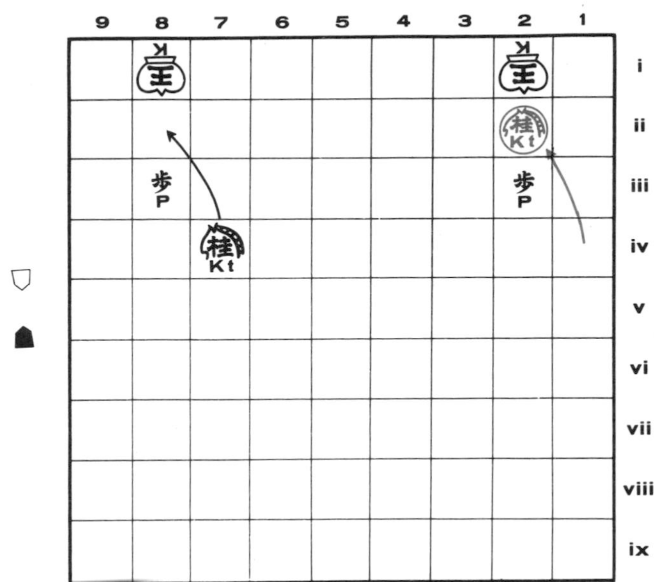

LEARNING TO USE THE PIECES

Left: You are in position for a mate.

Right: You have made the mate by advancing your Knight to the square in front of the King and promoting it to Gold.

Your new Gold now threatens (checks) the King.

The King cannot take it because then the Pawn would take him.

Lastly, the King cannot go to either side, or diagonally forward, because then the Gold would take him just the same.

It is checkmate, and the game stops here, when the King is checked and cannot escape.

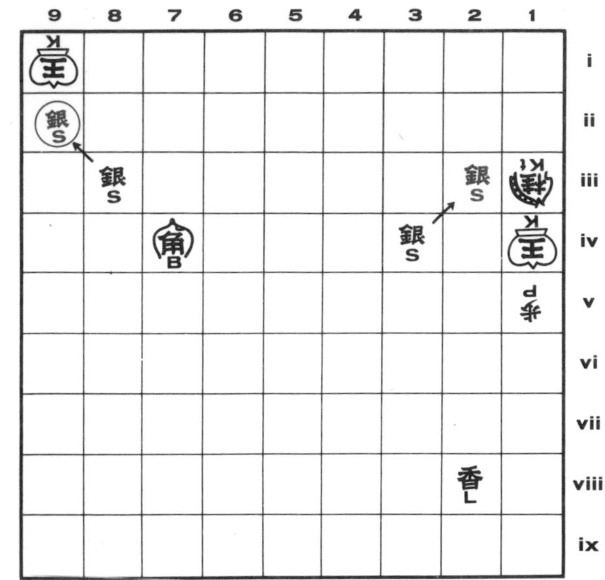

Left: The Silver goes to 9 ii where it is promoted to Gold and mates.

The King cannot take the new Gold because it is protected by the Bishop, whose power extends right along the diagonal.

Note that if the Silver does not promote, the King would escape by slipping out to 8 ii.

Right: Here the Silver mates *by not promoting.*

He does not promote because he needs to keep his Silver power of striking back along the rear diagonal.

The King cannot come out because of the Lance on 2 viii, which also of course protects the Silver so that the King cannot take it.

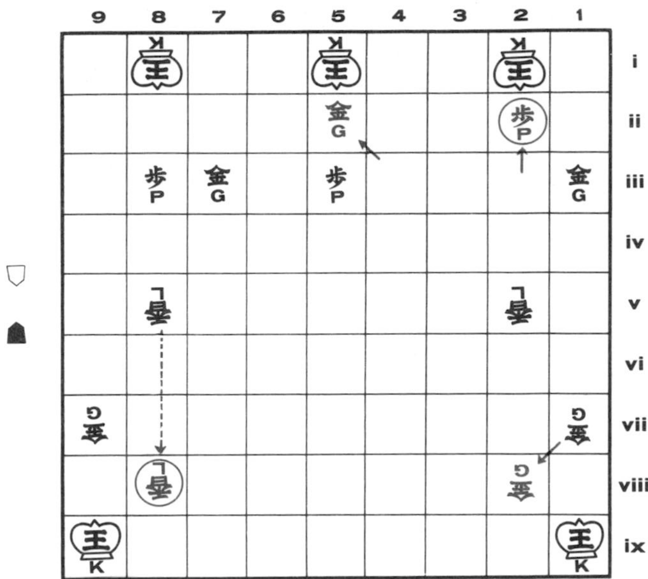

Top Left: In position for a mate. The Pawn is sitting over the King, and the Gold is beside it.

Top Middle: One way of making this mate. The Gold moves in front of the King, checking him and covering all his escape squares at the same time.

The Gold cannot be taken because he is protected by the Pawn.

Top Right: The other way of making the mate is to leave the Gold where it is and move the Pawn forward, promoting it to Gold (its whole move being made beyond the promotion line).

Here the Gold stays where it is as the protecting piece, and the promoted Pawn gives the mate.

Bottom Left: A mate with Gold and Lance. The Gold is sitting over the King, and the Lance comes shooting down the file till it gets to 8 viii, where it promotes to Gold and mates the King.

Bottom Right: The same pieces, but the mate made another way.

The Lance stays back to give protection, and the Gold moves up to give the mate.

Note that the Gold here must move to 2 viii, where it will be supported by the Lance. If the Gold moved to 1 viii, it would be taken by the King.

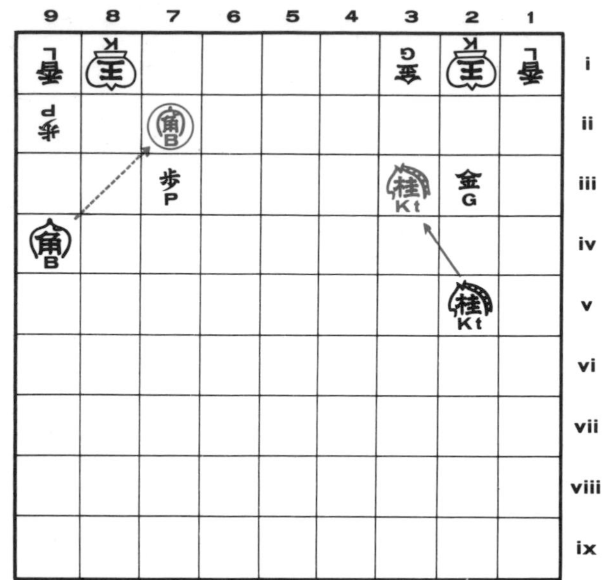

Left: The Bishop mates *by promoting.*

He checks the King with his original power as Bishop, namely along the diagonals. But now that he is promoted, he also has one square along the straight lines, and this extra power covers the King's escape squares 7 i and 8 ii.

The Bishop cannot be taken because he is protected by the Pawn. (The mate could also have been made by promoting the Pawn.)

Right: The Knight mates *by not promoting.*

Remember that if he promoted he would lose his original move and become merely a Gold. In this position, as a Gold he could not reach the King, whereas by remaining an unpromoted Knight he checks. Here his check is mate because all the King's flight squares are covered by the Gold on 2 iii.

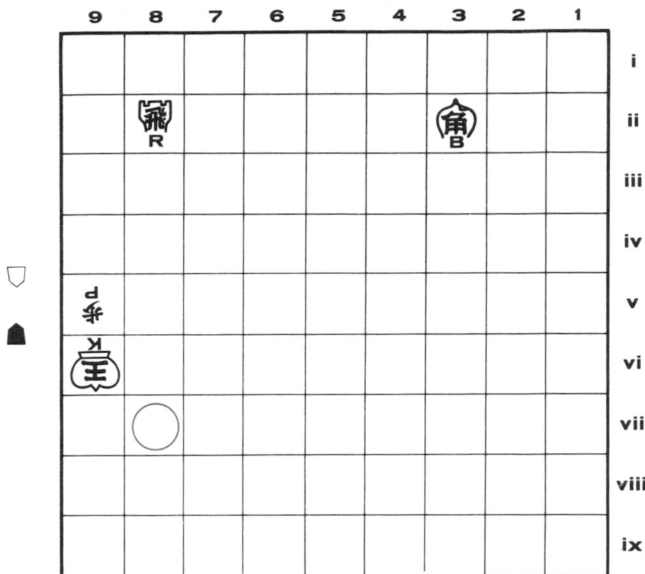

Here either the Bishop or the Rook can mate, by promoting and coming back from beyond the promotion line.

The key square is 8 vii.

The promotion is necessary in each case:

for the *Rook,* because he needs the diagonal one-square addition to his powers in order to check the King, which is on the diagonal from 8 vii,

for the *Bishop,* because if he does not promote he will give only a harmless check, and the King would escape to 9 vii. Whereas if he promotes, he covers this last square with his extra one square along the horizontal line.

Remember that the Rook and the Bishop keep all their original powers when they promote. The other pieces all lose their original nature, so to speak, and merely become Golds. So you *always* promote Rook and Bishop when you can, because you lose nothing and their powers increase. With the other pieces you must consider before promoting them whether it will be more useful to have the new Gold than to have the piece in its original role.

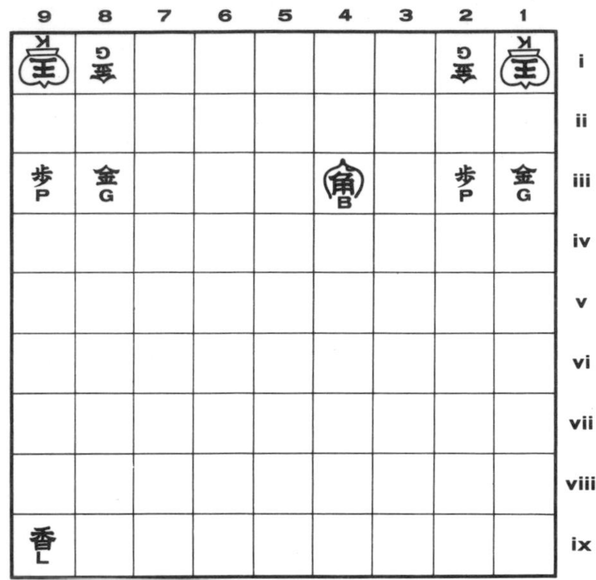

Simple Exchanging Combinations:

Left: You are in a mating position, thanks to the power of your Lance on 9 ix.

You play your Gold to 9 ii, giving check.

He must take it with his Gold.

Now you mate by taking his Gold with your Pawn, promoting to Gold and mating. He cannot take your promoted Pawn because it is protected by the Lance.

You could also makc this mate by first playing the Pawn to 9 ii and promoting it to Gold, and then when he takes, mate by retaking with your Gold, or even with your Lance (promoting it to Gold).

Right: You cannot mate directly on 2 ii because he would take your piece with his Gold. If you retook, his King would capture your last attacking piece.

So first of all you knock out his defender, the Gold on 2 i. You play your Bishop to 2 i, taking the Gold and promoting. Your Bishop now checks him with its promoted power, and he must take it with his King.

His King has lost its defending bodyguard, and you mate on 2 ii with Gold or promoted Pawn.

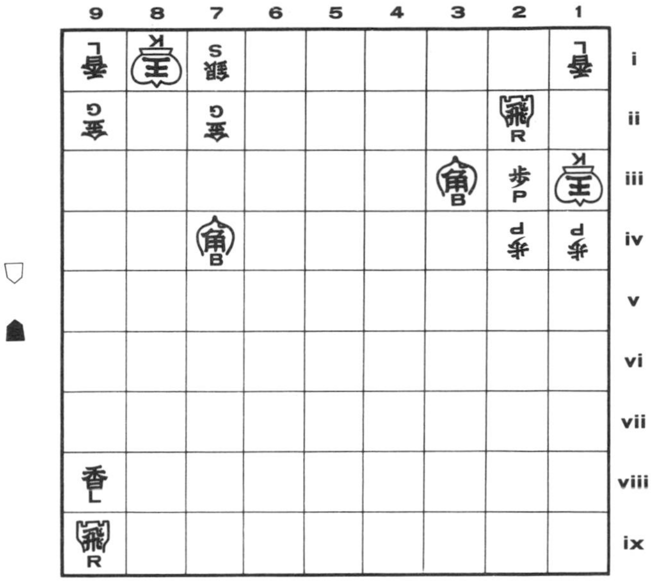

Left: You can win in any order. The key square is 9 ii.

You take his Gold on 9 ii with either your Bishop or your Lance, promoting in either case.

He must now take with his Lance or he is mate.

You retake his Lance, again promoting, and this move mates him.

Right: A Tiny Problem.

You have your two big pieces for the attack, and it is clear that you will win if you simply move the Rook down to 2 i and promote.

But the rule in Shogi problems is that *every move must be check.* How do you mate him in two moves, every move being a check?

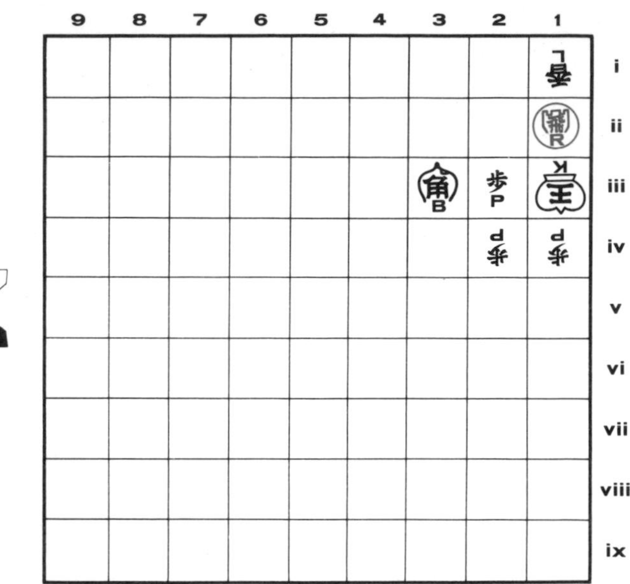

The Key move of the problem is to play your Rook to 1 ii, promoting. Now he has to take it.

The opponent can take this either with his King or his Lance.

Suppose he takes it with the King. . . .

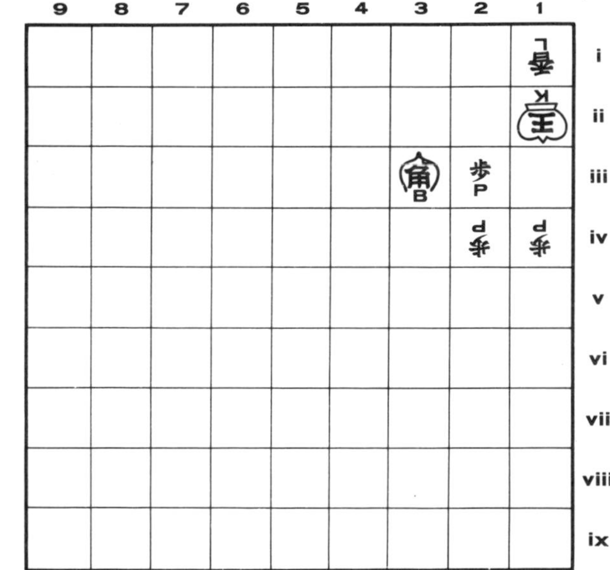

What you have achieved is to get your Rook out of the way and off the mating square, 2 ii. Your Bishop is now free to play to that square. . . .

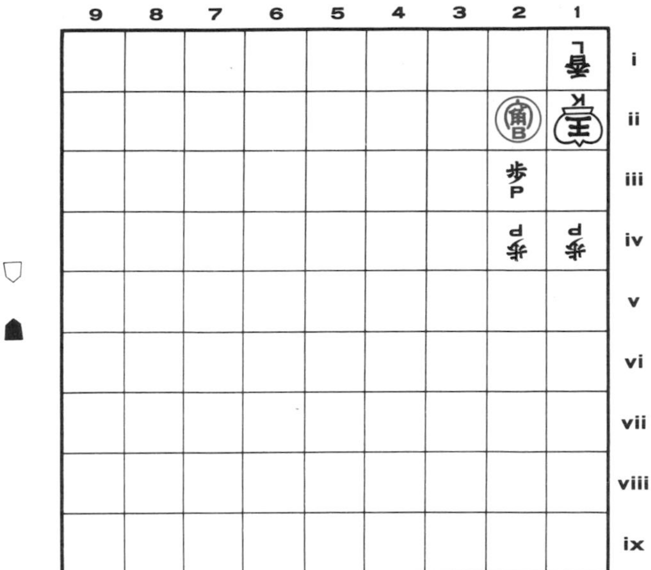

. . . to give the mate. Note that he *must promote* to checkmate the King because he needs both the straight and diagonal lines to cover all the King's possible escape squares.

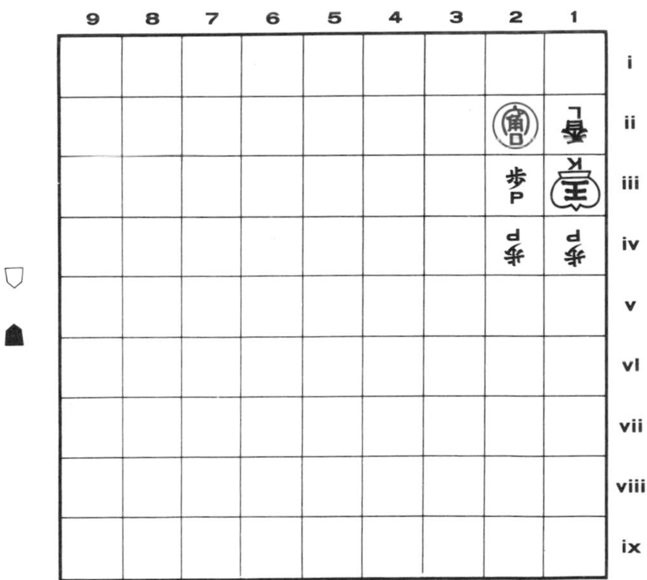

If your opponent had taken the Rook with his Lance, your Bishop would mate him just the same. The Bishop is protected by the Pawn, and in turn the Bishop (with its promotion powers) protects the Pawn from being captured by the King.

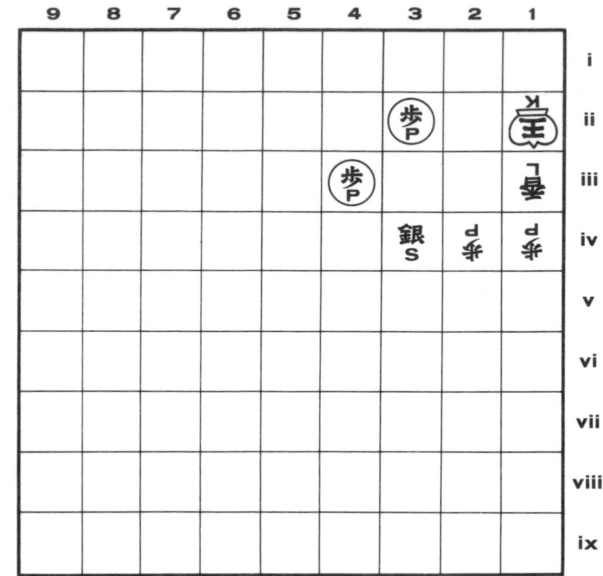

Smothering With Two Golds.

This is an important end-play which frequently occurs in actual games. It is essential that you should be able to recognize it when it comes up in one form or another. Later on, of course, you must be able to foresee it well ahead and either bring it about or move to avoid it, as the case may be.

As this is a problem, you have to give checkmate by checking with every move. You have two promoted Pawns (in other words, two Golds) which are not quite close enough to mate. If you had one spare move, you could bring up your promoted Pawn from 4 iii to 3 iii and then finish him off in a number of ways.

This gives you the clue. Somehow you must manage it so that you can make that move and give check at the same time.

(A little experiment will convince you that a sacrifice on 2 ii is useless—your remaining pieces are still too far away.)

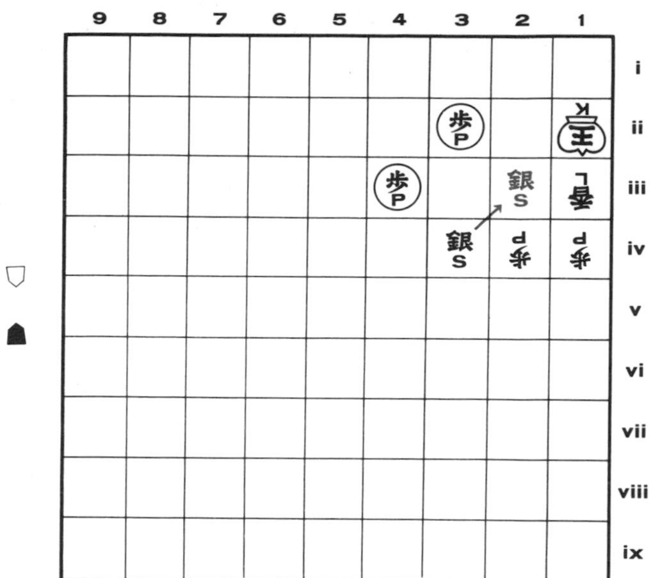

Here is your solution—you play your Silver to 2 iii, giving check. If he does not take it but plays King–1 i, then you mate easily with Silver–2 ii (promotes).

So he must take your Silver: King–2 iii.

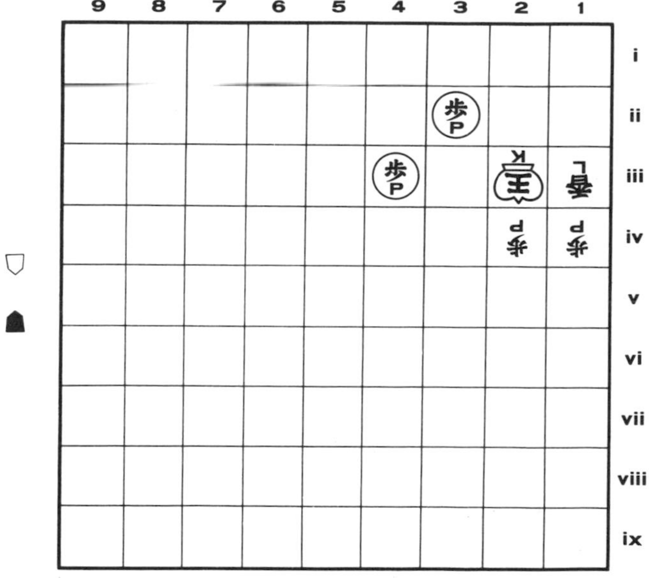

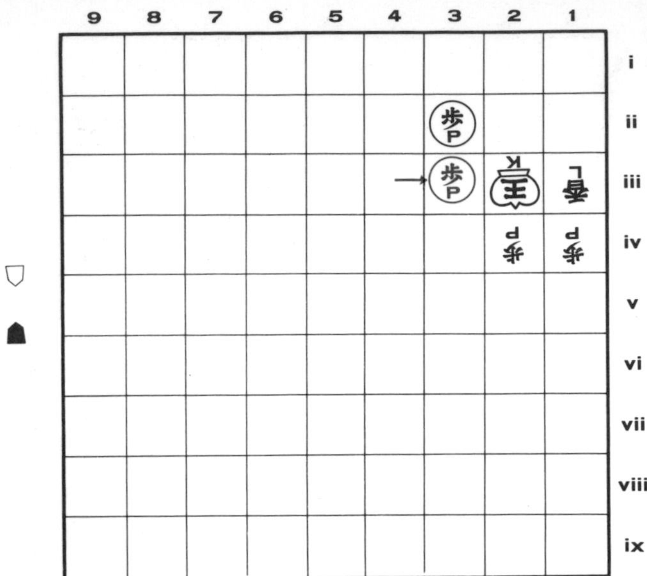

You close in with your promoted Pawn, which is a Gold. The two Golds protect each other, and the King cannot take either of them. He has to go back to 1 ii.

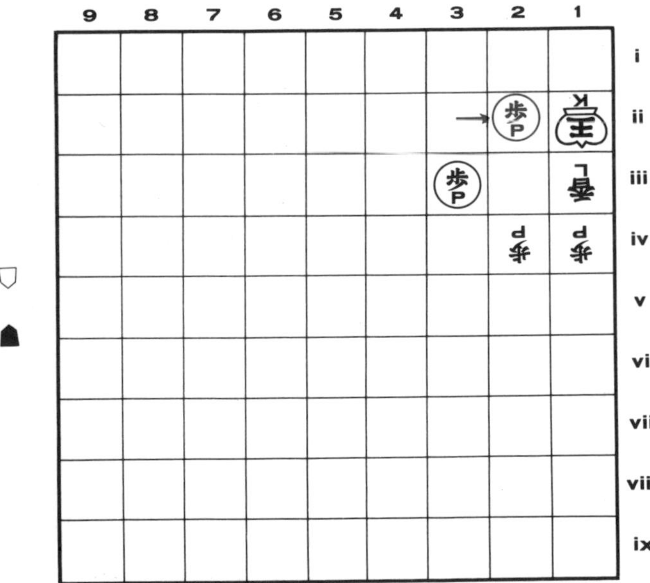

You have smothered the King with the two Golds and give the mate on 2 ii with either of them.

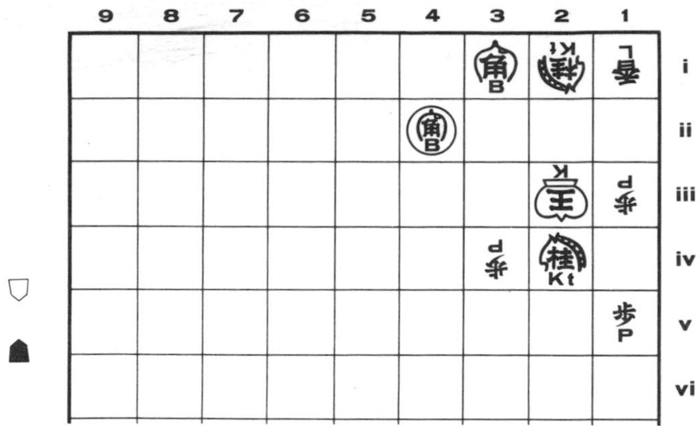

Another small problem: You have two Bishops, one of them promoted (never mind why and how for the moment—this is just an exercise.)

You would like to move the promoted one to 3 ii to mate, but then the King would take your Knight. So how to mate him in two moves? You should be able to solve this one without looking at the solution. . . .

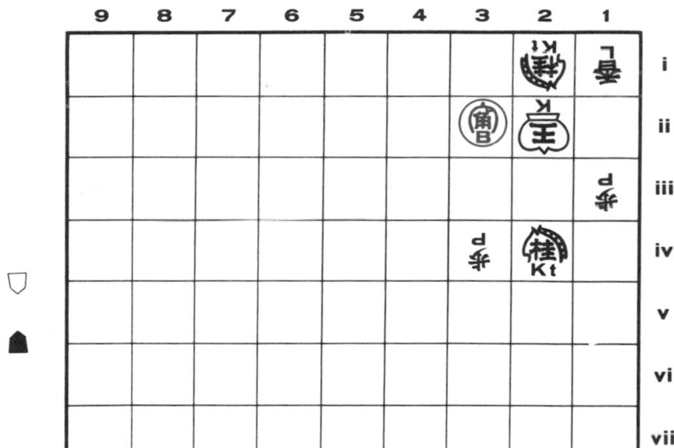

The solution is: Bishop to 2 ii, promoting and checking. The King must take this piece. Then your promoted Bishop goes to 3 ii and mates, as the King has now been drawn away from the undefended Knight. In notation it would look like this:

B–2 ii (promotes) K–same (square)
pr. B–3 ii mate

Shogi books don't write in the "check!"—you are expected to see it. The "K to same" is the standard way of writing, which I keep because it will make it easier to go on to Shogi scores later.

Here your opponent seems well guarded. If you check him with your Bishop on 3 iv, which looks the natural move, he slides his Gold up to interpose. You could take with your Silver, but his Lance on 2 i would re-take and your attack has failed.

You have to mate here in *two moves,* each move a check. (As a matter of fact, B–3 iv does finally mate, but in three moves, not two.)

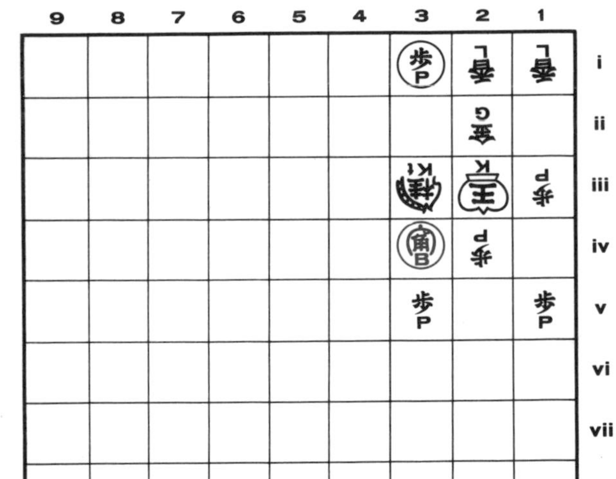

The solution is Silver–2 iii. He can take with either his Gold or his King. If he takes with the Gold, your Bishop promotes on 2 i and mates. If he takes with the King, you have a pretty mate on 3 iv, reminiscent of a chess end-game study.

THE PARATROOPS

NOW that you have an idea of how the pieces work, it is time to introduce you to a revolutionary feature of Shogi, found in no other form of chess. This is the "drop"—a sort of paratroop attack.

When you capture an enemy, it is not dead.

It becomes yours and you keep it by the side of the board.

Any time, instead of a move, you can drop one of these captured men on any vacant square. The piece now points towards the enemy, and it is your piece and works for you.

First one or two examples of how this works in practice.

1. In this position, you take his Gold with your Rook. The Rook is promoted, and the King must recapture.

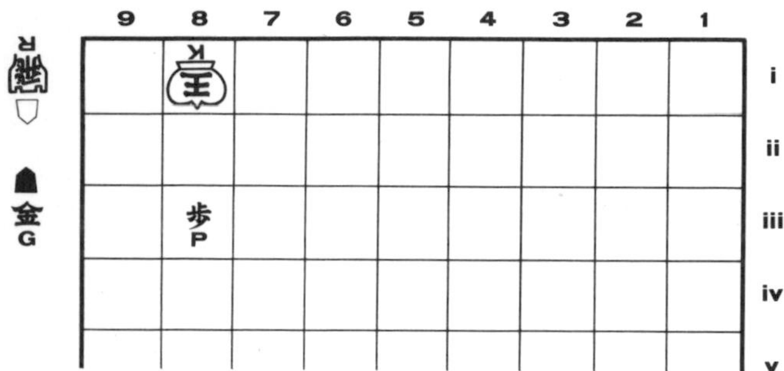

2. The Gold is now *yours,* and it is shown at the side of the board. The Rook is *his.*

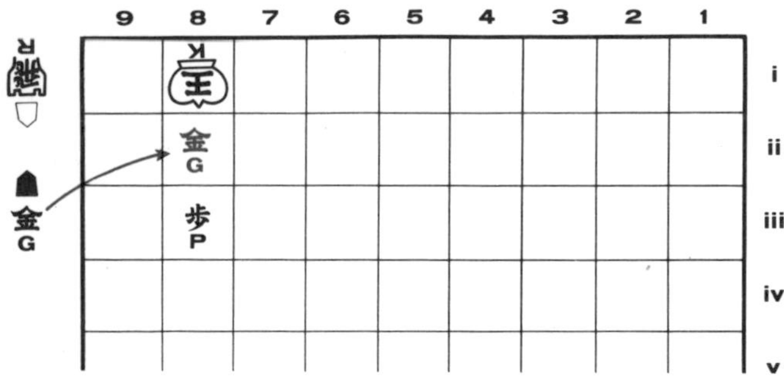

3. It is your move again, after his King captures the Rook. Instead of moving a piece on the board, you "drop" your Gold in hand in front of his King, where it is protected by the Pawn. He is mated and has no chance to use his "Rook in hand."

In notation: R–8 i (promotes)

K–same

G drops 8 ii (mate)

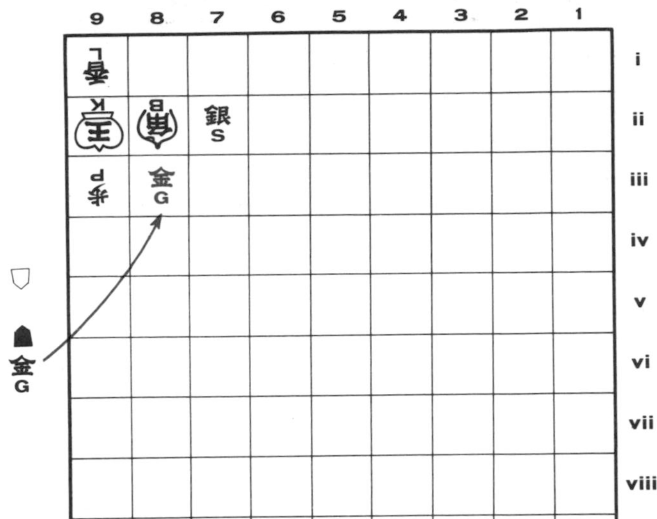

You have a Gold in hand. Perhaps you have had it for some time and have been awaiting the right moment. It has now come, and you can mate.

G drops 8 iii (mate)

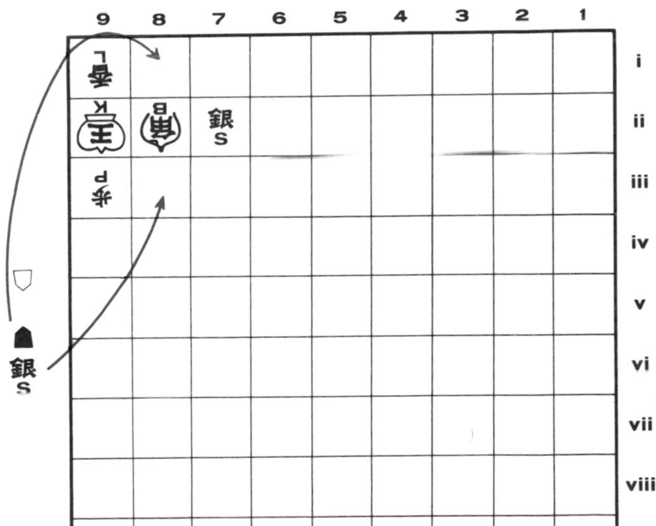

If it had been a Silver in hand, even better. You have a choice of two squares for your mate.

S drops 8 i, or
S drops 8 iii

In either case it is decisive. A Bishop would mate similarly.

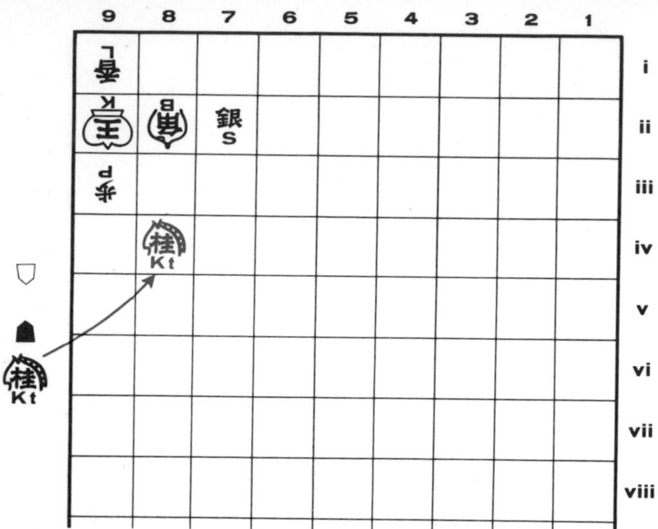

Try a Knight in the same position. The key square then is 8 iv.

Note that you could not make this mate by dropping any piece other than these four: Gold, Silver, Bishop, or Knight.

You cannot drop a piece and promote as you drop, even if it is beyond the promotion line.

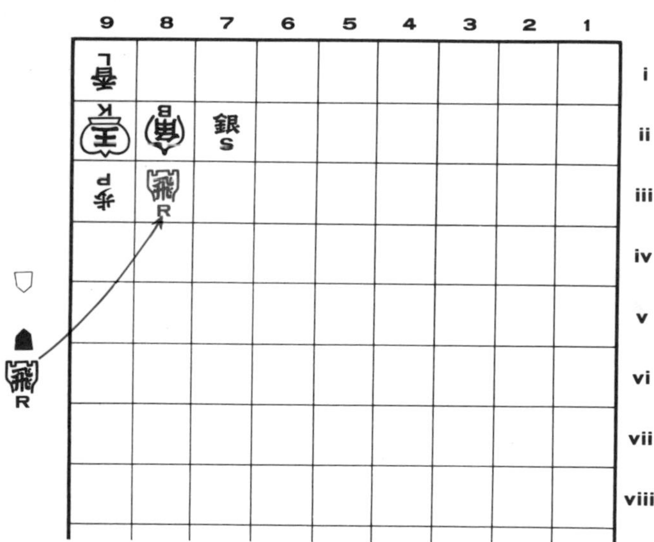

No mate here. The Rook (and it would be the same with a Lance or a Pawn) has to drop *as itself.* It cannot promote till it makes a move *on the board.* And that move, of course, must be wholly or partly beyond the promotion line.

There are two restrictions on Pawn drops, which you must know:

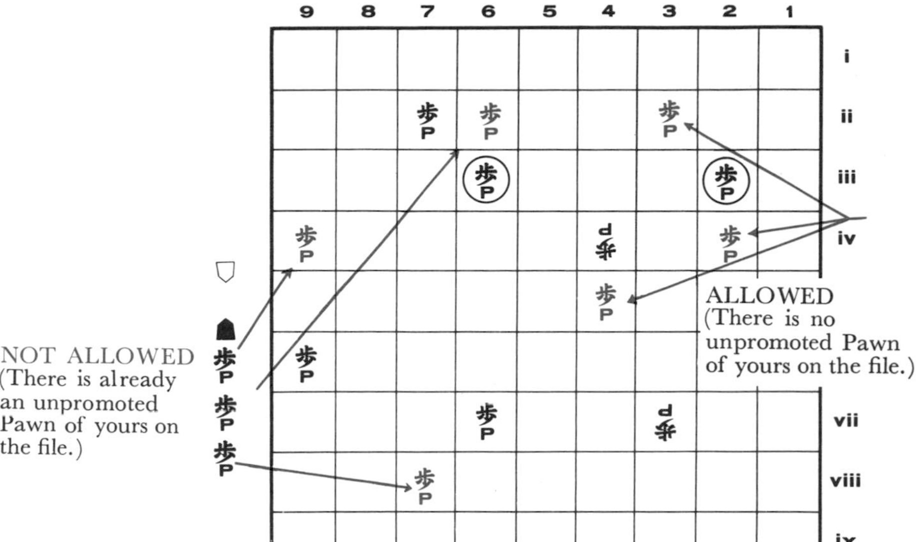

Rule 1: You may not drop a second Pawn on a file where you already have a Pawn, unless that one has been promoted.

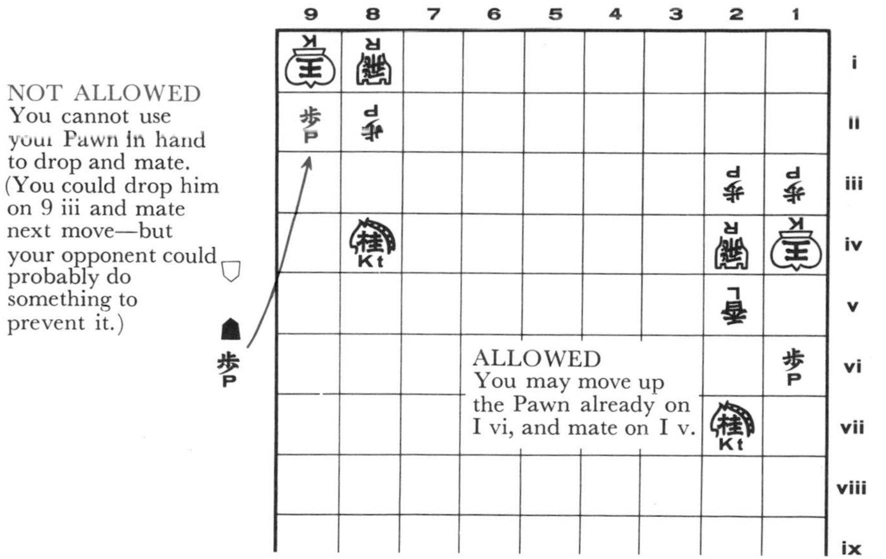

Rule 2: You may not give mate by dropping a Pawn in front of the enemy King.

But you may give mate by moving up a Pawn already on the board.

There are a few other minor restrictions which hardly concern beginners. You mustn't drop a piece so that it can never move again —that's to say you mustn't drop a Pawn or a Lance on the last rank, or a Knight on the last two ranks. The reason is that they can't make their normal move, and they can't be promoted until they have made at least one move as themselves.

The paratroops are a constant source of Shogi "shocks," especially to Westerners brought up on chess. We show here a few important attacking drops, apart from mating combinations.

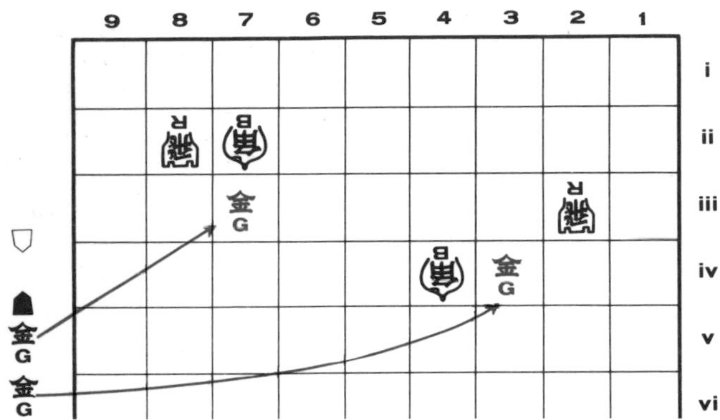

The Gold threatens Rook and Bishop if close together.

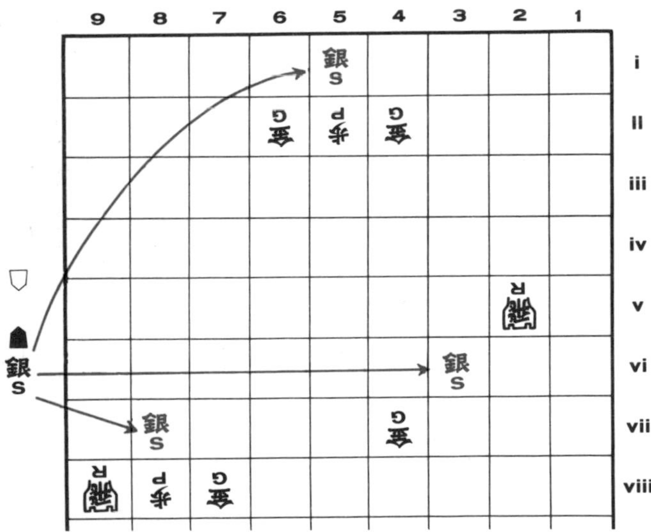

The Silver frequently forks two Golds, or Gold and Rook.

As you see in the above three cases, either the Rook or one Gold is lost. The attacked pieces cannot move to protect each other.

The Bishops, when in hand after being exchanged, can make devastating "forks" which must be constantly watched.

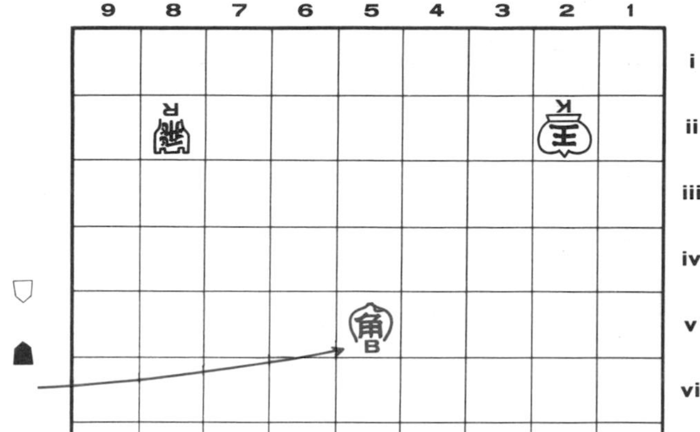

The Bishop fork: The Bishop has been dropped on 5 v (frequently the square of doom) where he checks the King and attacks the Rook at the same time. When the check is avoided, he takes the Rook in the next move.

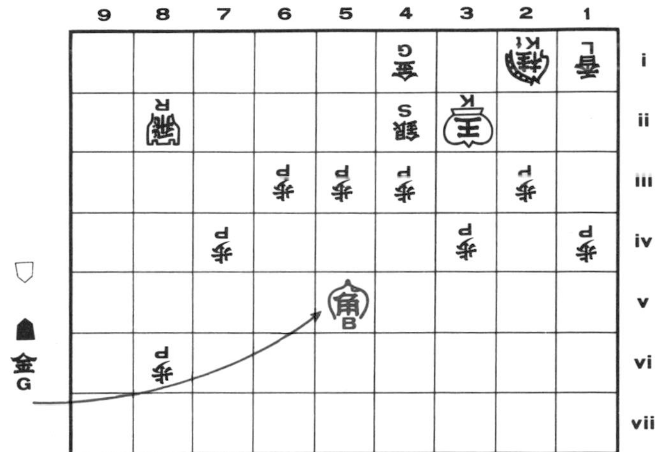

The expert drops the Bishop, not the Gold.

Here is the fork as it might appear in an actual game. The beginner is tempted to drop his Gold on 2 ii, forcing the King to take it. Then the King is in line for the fork, and the beginner now drops his Bishop on 5 v. He has won a Rook for a Gold.

But the more expert player makes a far better move. He plays directly Bishop–5 v. He threatens to give *mate* by dropping his Gold onto 2 ii. The opponent must defend (probably by moving his Silver up to 3 iii), and then the Rook is won for nothing, a much better transaction.

As in chess, the Knight is a great one for forks. There is a saying: "If you have two Knights in hand, never despair," and indeed they can pull you out of some seemingly hopeless positions.

The first Knight drops onto 9 v, giving check and forcing the King back to 8 ii. (If he came up to 9 iv, the second Knight would mate from 8 vi.) Now the other Knight drops onto 7 iv, forking King and Rook.

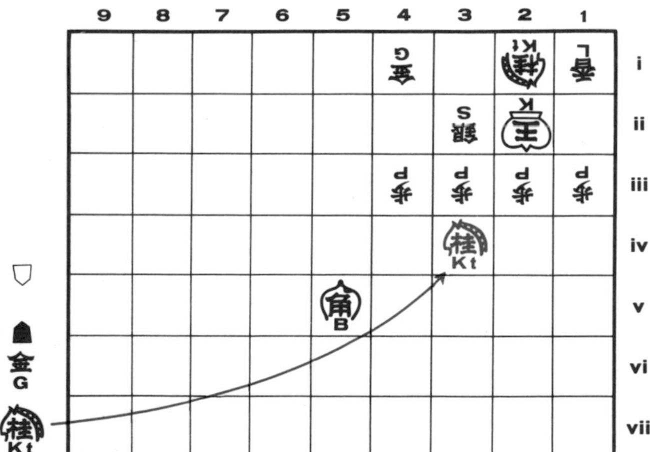

The Knight combines with a Gold in hand to give a snappy and unexpected mate. Watch out for this both as defender and attacker, for it is a possibility which frequently occurs.

The Knight drops and checks the King, and then the Gold dropped on 2 ii gives the mate. Note that the Knight cannot be taken by the Pawn because the latter is pinned, defending the King, by the Bishop. There are many variations of this neat little mate.

THE VALUE OF THE PIECES

JUST a brief note here on the value of the pieces, as a general aid to the beginner. Of course in special positions, pieces have special values—if you can mate with one move by dropping a Knight, and in no other way, then a Knight is to you the most valuable piece on the board! What we say here is to give you an idea, when exchanging in positions where there is no special attack, of the likely value of the pieces to you in the future. (Of course you also need to consider counter drops by the enemy, using exchanged pieces.)

The *Rook* is the strongest piece on the board, and the further you get into the middle and end of the game, the stronger he gets. Only in the opening, when as yet few pieces have been exchanged and there are few open lines, does the Rook fail to shine. If you give up your Rook, you should aim to get not less than three pieces for it, or else a Bishop plus one other piece.

The *Bishop* is not quite as strong as the Rook. It is most effective in the opening. To give up a Bishop you need to get at least two Golds or Silvers, and even then you often have the worst of the bargain. If you can take his Rook with your Bishop, it generally pays to do so.

The *Gold* and *Silver* are not too different in strength, but the Gold is in most positions slightly more powerful, especially in defense. If you can knock out his defending Gold by giving up a Silver, it is generally good to do so.

The *Knight* and *Lance* are definitely the "minor pieces" and are roughly equal in strength. Perhaps two of them are equal to one Gold. Remember they are almost useless in defense—if you are on the defensive, the Gold and Silver are most valuable. The Knight and Lance tend to be inactive until the game is well under way, and even then as a rule you only get one pair of them out. They are often victims of a foray by a promoted Bishop or Rook, and once captured, they come in with great force as paratroops in the middle of the board. If you have hopes of attack, it is worth while spending a move or two picking up an enemy Knight or Lance; they are very useful to reinforce an attack by paratroop drops. But if you are on the defensive, it is waste of time to acquire them. You do better to gather your Golds and Silvers round your King.

The *Pawns* have no real exchange value—generally the game finishes up with each of you having several Pawns in hand. Only in the opening, and in certain attacking positions, is the possession of an extra Pawn in hand a vital advantage. Never simply take Pawns for the sake of winning them, unless you can see clearly that you need them.

NOVICES' GAME

AS AN introduction to how the pieces work on a full board, we are going to show you a game between two almost complete novices—both of whom, however, could play chess, as it happened. Without bothering with many variations or principles, we shall point out just a few mistakes. Take note of these—their mistakes will be your mistakes, and to make progress you must improve your technique. Beginners tend to be satisfied with themselves when they have won a game; but generally it is because, as here, the opponent played worse.

Here is the board with the pieces set up: the Pawns are on the third rank; the Rook and Bishop have the second rank to themselves; the King and his bodyguard are on the back rank, flanked by the Knights and Lances.

Black is this side, with the first move, and White faces him.

The two marks, black and white, by the side of the board are to show the "hand" where the captured men are kept ready to be dropped as opportunity arises.

A common opening is to advance the Pawn in front of the Rook, with two objects:

(1) to mobilize the Rook and give it a free line, hoping ultimately to break through into the enemy camp;

(2) to exchange off a Pawn and so get at least one Pawn in hand.

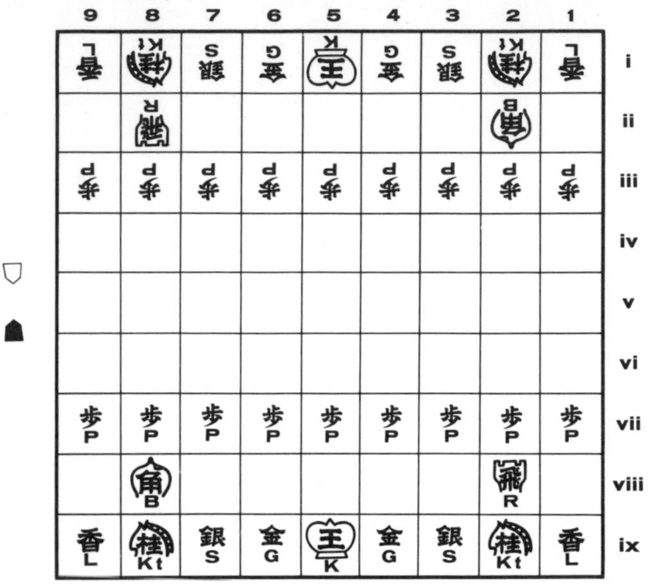

9	8	7	6	5	4	3	2	1	
香 L	桂 Kt	銀 S	金 G	王 K	金 G	銀 S	桂 Kt	香 L	i
	飛 R						角 B		ii
歩 P	歩 P	歩 P	歩 P	歩 P	歩 P	歩 P	歩 P	歩 P	iii
									iv
									v
									vi
歩 P	歩 P	歩 P	歩 P	歩 P	歩 P	歩 P	歩 P	歩 P	vii
	角 B						飛 R		viii
香 L	桂 Kt	銀 S	金 G	王 K	金 G	銀 S	桂 Kt	香 L	ix

You are taking the part of Black, and your idea is to push your Pawn on 2 vii forward. We shall number the moves, and from now on will use the Japanese form of notation—that is, the square first, and then the piece to be moved onto it. So 2 vi P means that onto the square 2 vi you move a Pawn. There is of course only one Pawn which can move onto that square.

	Black	White
1.	2 vi P	. . . 8 iv P Your opponent has the same idea.
2.	2 v P	. . . 7 ii S He intends to bring out his Silver; the idea is not wrong, but he ought first to protect his weak point, 2 iii.
3.	2 iv P	. . . Same Pawn His Pawn moves to the same square to capture yours, otherwise your Pawn will promote on 2 iii and become a Gold right in his camp.

Your opponent has just captured your Pawn on 2 iv (diagram). So he now has a Pawn in hand, and it is shown by his side of the board. Note that at the moment he cannot drop that Pawn anywhere on the board, because on all of the files he already has a Pawn.

See that if *you* had a Pawn in hand, you could immediately win

	9	8	7	6	5	4	3	2	1	
	香 L	桂 Kt		金 G	王 K	金 G	銀 S	桂 Kt	香 L	i
		飛 R	銀 S					角 B		ii
	歩 P		歩 P	歩 P	歩 P	歩 P	歩 P		歩 P	iii
☖ 歩 P		歩 P						歩 P		iv
										v
☗										vi
	歩 P	歩 P	歩 P	歩 P	歩 P	歩 P	歩 P		歩 P	vii
		角 B						飛 R		viii
	香 L	桂 Kt	銀 S	金 G	王 K	金 G	銀 S	桂 Kt	香 L	ix

his Bishop by dropping the Pawn on 2 iii. But you have not, so you proceed to get one by capturing—

BLACK WHITE

4. Same Rook

That means you play your Rook to the same square to which the opponent has just played. In doing so, you capture his Pawn. Now you too have a Pawn in hand. He must do something to prevent your trapping his Bishop by dropping your Pawn on 2 iii (which you can do because you have no other Pawn on that file). So he plays:

. . . 3 iv P

letting out the Bishop.

You could capture this Pawn with your Rook, but it is tricky for a beginner to do so because an unpromoted Rook easily gets tied up, trapped, and captured once it gets off the open file.

5. 2 viii R

The idea is to vacate the point 2 iv in order to drop the Pawn there and in the next move promote it on 2 iii. To drop it straight away onto 2 iii is not so good because it cannot promote as it drops. The Bishop will move away in any case, and from 2 iii the Pawn can only advance onto the heavily protected square 2 ii where it will capture nothing and will itself be taken.

To promote your Rook on 2 iii looks attractive, but it would get in the way of your scheme of promoting a Pawn. In fact he would drive your promoted Rook away with 3 ii G, and then "put up the bars" by dropping his Pawn on 2 iii, which would shut you out for a long time to come.

. . . 3 ii G

He plays it anyway, not seeing the danger.

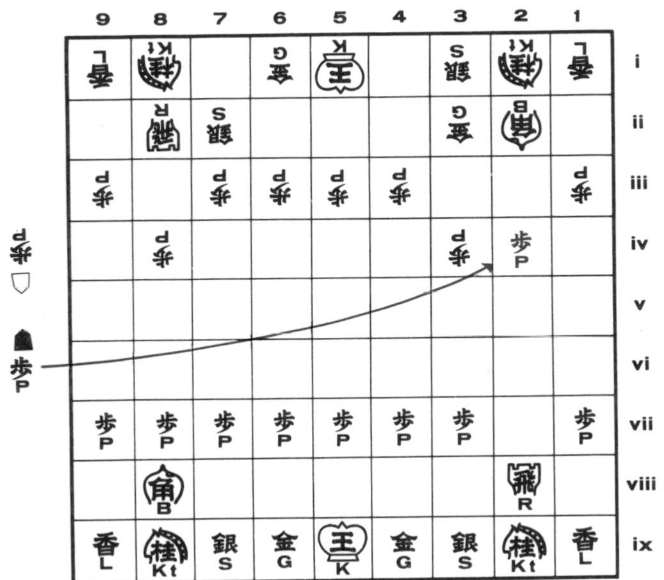

6. 2 iv P drops (diagram)

Your opponent obviously did not expect this powerful move. He probably thought you meant to drop on 2 iii, in which case he would simply move his Bishop away and be safe for the time being. Now he cannot prevent your promoting this dropped Pawn to a Gold.

. . . 5 v B

He gets at least the Bishop out of danger.

7. 2 iii P (promotes)

You now have a promoted Pawn right amongst his pieces. He will surely move his Gold away. Remember that if he exchanges it against your promoted Pawn, all he gets in hand will be a Pawn, because when captured it reverts to its original status. Whereas on your side you get a full Gold to drop anywhere.

. . . 4 ii G (diagram)

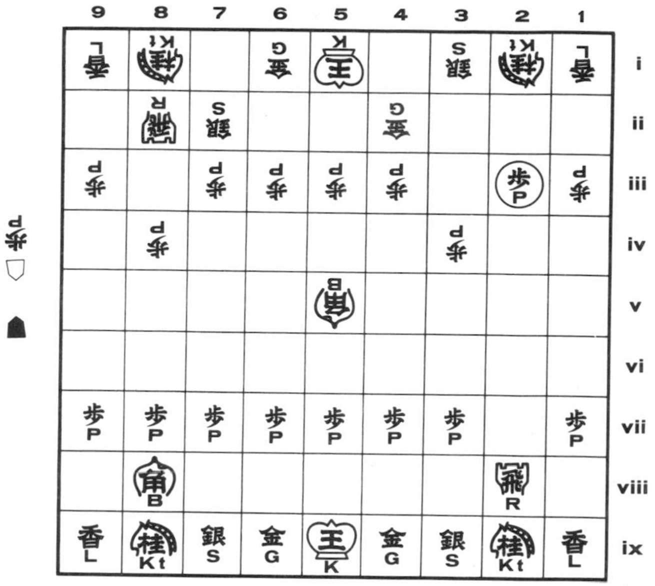

White's idea is to play to shut you out by dropping his Pawn in hand onto 2 ii. You could not take it with your promoted Pawn because that square is well protected. Nor could you do anything except make a rather feeble retreat to 2 iv. You must do something quickly before he shuts you out with this move.

8. 1 ii pr. P

This looks good because your promoted Pawn (now of course a Gold) attacks both his Lance and Knight, and he must take it. Then the line for your Rook is open.

. . . Same Lance

His Lance moves to the square to which you just moved, namely 1 ii, capturing your promoted Pawn. It now goes into his hand but only, remember, as a simple Pawn. It loses its promoted status.

9. 2 i R (promotes)

As you move to 2 i, you capture his Knight which is on that square, and you promote your Rook at the same time. You threaten to take either his Lance or his Silver on the next move. He decides to protect his Silver, the more valuable of the two.

. . . 3 ii G (diagram)

Obviously your opponent's strategy has been very wrong, since he has to keep moving this piece to and fro in order to hold his game together.

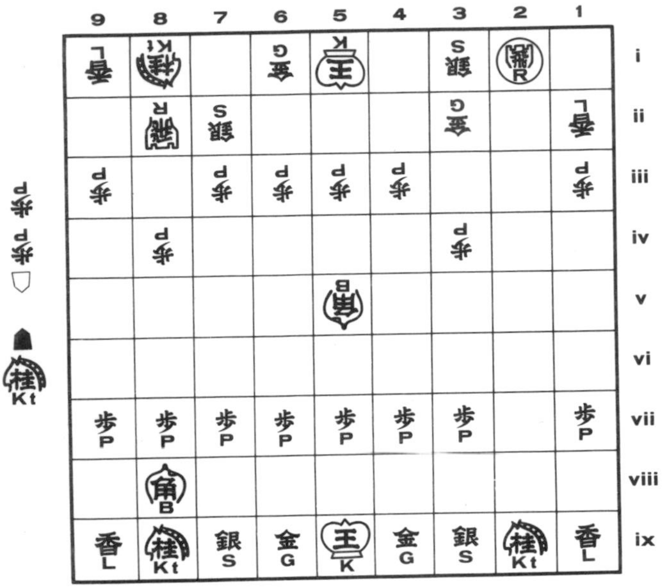

You have a clear advantage in position and material.

You have, however, so far played with just two of your pieces, and the only reason you succeed in this game is that your opponent's strategy has been even worse. He shut off his Rook by playing the Silver to 7 ii, and he failed to see how you would break through on file 2 and so did not get his Gold to 3 ii in time to shut you out.

Long ago you should have played 7 vi P, exchanging Bishops if necessary. Then you should have brought your King to safety on the left, accompanied by at least two Golds. Lastly you could have sent a Silver up the file to help your Rook break through on 2 iii.

You will see these things illustrated when we come to the expert games later on; here they are just pointed out.

We return to the actual game. You now make a typical novice's move, ingenious and enterprising, but over-ambitious.

10. 2 iii Kt drops (diagram)

You attack his Silver, which cannot move away because your Rook would then take his King. In other words, the Silver is pinned.

Perhaps an expert would here play 2 ii B, trying to cut his losses, but your opponent sees that he can take the Knight.

. . . Same G

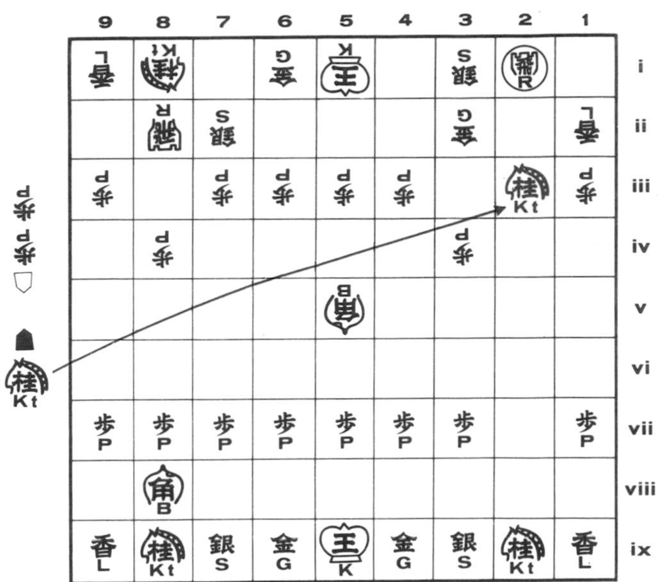

11. 3 i pr. R

You play your promoted Rook to 3 i, taking his Silver and giving check. This is stronger than taking the Gold or the Lance. As his King is in check, he must move or interpose.

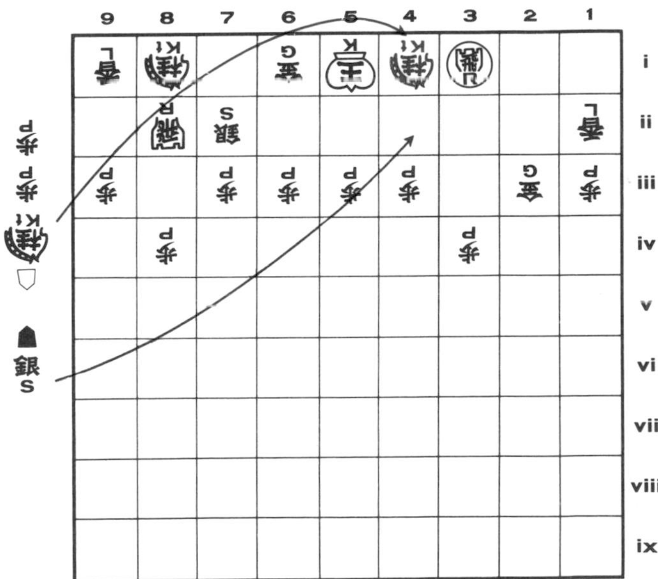

We spend a page here to show what happens if he interposes. He cannot interpose one of the Pawns in hand, because he has already a Pawn on file 4. But he could drop his Knight, which he captured from you on the previous move, on 4 i.

Suppose then that he puts in the Knight by dropping it on 4 i (diagram). This seems to seal off your attack.

But as a matter of fact, you immediately win the Knight by dropping your Silver in hand onto 4 ii. This checks him, and he cannot take the Silver with his King because it is protected by your promoted Rook. Therefore he has to move away.

Then you take his defenseless Knight, either with the promoted Rook or with the Silver. The latter would be stronger because you then threaten another check with 4 ii R.

Have a good look at this method of attacking in which the dropped piece works with a promoted Rook already on the board. It very frequently occurs in Shogi combinations.

	9	8	7	6	5	4	3	2	1
i	香 L	桂 Kt		金 G	王 K		龍 R		
ii		龍 R	銀 S						香 L
iii	歩 P		歩 P	歩 P	歩 P	歩 P		金 G	歩 P
iv		歩 P					歩 P		
v					馬 B				
vi									
vii	歩 P	歩 P	歩 P	歩 P	歩 P	歩 P	歩 P		歩 P
viii		角 B							
ix	香 L	桂 Kt	銀 S	金 G	王 K	金 G	銀 S	桂 Kt	香 L

☖ 桂 Kt 歩 P 歩 P

☗ 銀 S

We go back to the original game, with your promoted Rook checking his King (diagram). We have seen that he cannot interpose his Knight without losing it, so he moves away.

. . . 6 ii K

12. 7 vi P

Good! At last you see that you cannot make much progress with just the two pieces, so you move your Pawn to 7 vi to open the line of the Bishop. You offer to exchange Bishops, in order to get another piece in hand.

Generally you need at least two pieces in hand if you have only one piece on the ground near his King. If you have two active men on the ground, you may be able to mate with only one piece to drop.

. . . 8 viii B

He exchanges Bishops rather than retreat—also he sees a chance of a combination.

13. Same S

You retake with your Silver as planned. To help in your attack you have added a full Bishop to your piece already in hand. But so of course has he. Your opponent plays:

. . . 2 ii B drops (diagram)

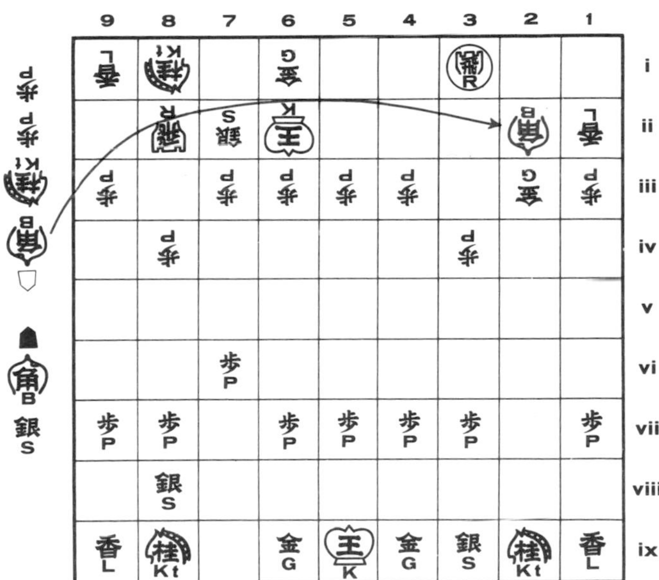

This is one of those shocks that you are always likely to get when the Bishops are "wild." He attacks your promoted Rook from close quarters, and at the same time threatens your undefended Silver on 8 viii. If you protect or move one, he takes the other. If you take his Bishop with your Rook, he retakes with the Gold and your last attacking piece on the board has vanished.

It is a working rule that in *normal positions* (i.e. where the enemy King has at least a couple of pieces as bodyguards), *you cannot launch a successful attack by paratroop drops alone.* Your pieces simply get gobbled up as they come down. *You must have at least one piece already on the board near the opposing King* before you can begin successful paratroop drops.

So here, if you exchange your Rook, your chance of attack goes. To gain time, you give check:

14. 4 ii R

Now if he would just move away his King, you get the time to bring your Silver to safety on the protected square 7 vii. But your opponent does not mean to let you off. Keeping up the pressure, he plays:

. . . 5 ii G

He attacks your Rook again, this time with the Gold. Your Silver is still in peril. If you take his Bishop, your last attacking chance disappears, as explained before. You temporize with another check:

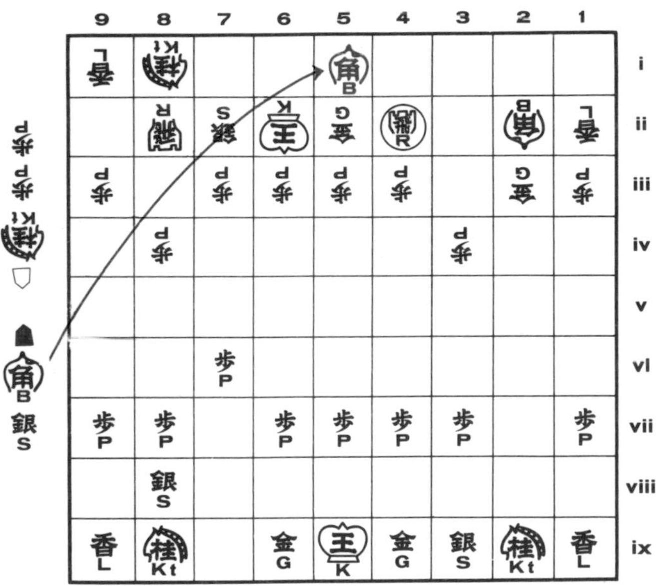

15. 5 i B drops

Your opponent finds this check troublesome. He does not want to leave his Gold unprotected, because then your Rook could take it for nothing.

He cannot take your Bishop, which is protected by the promoted Rook, so he has to move his King, and he moves to 6 i in order to keep in touch with the Gold and protect it with his King.

The Bishop check which you have made is basically the same.

maneuver which was explained on page 39; it is very strong and typical of many Shogi attacks.

Your opponent, then, moves his King:

. . . 6 i K

Suddenly you perceive that you have got him! You can finish off the game by mating him in two moves, two of *your* moves, that is. (The Japanese count each move separately, yours and his, so they would say it is a mate in three moves.)

Try to work this out before you look at the answer.

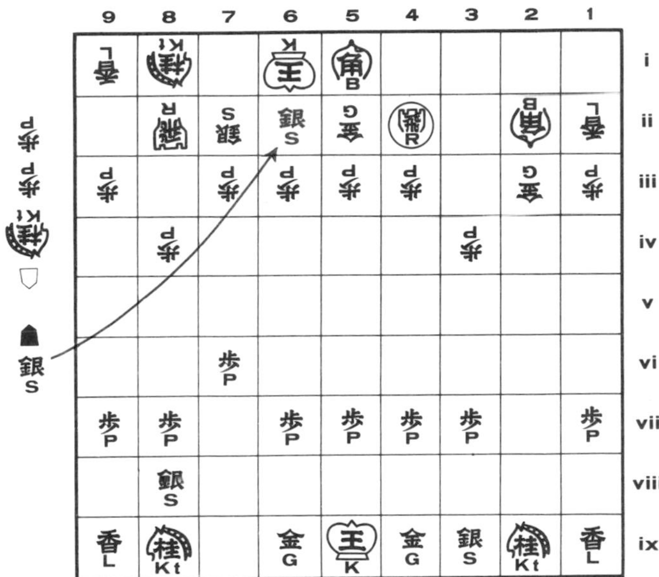

16. 6 ii S drops (diagram)

This drop checks him. He cannot move away because the only vacant square is 7 i which is equally covered by the Silver.

He cannot take the Silver with his King because it is protected by your Bishop. So he has only one move, to take it with his Gold on 5 ii.

. . . Same G

17. Same B (promotes)—mate

Final Position

Here is the final position. You could also have mated on the last move by taking the Gold with your promoted Rook.

Well, strategically the game was not impressive—almost all your pieces are still on their original squares—but you managed the final combination quite neatly, and the play will have given you a little insight into how the pieces work. We chose a game between beginners because the play is with only a few pieces and is therefore less confusing as an introduction. But now you have to learn to play with the whole board.

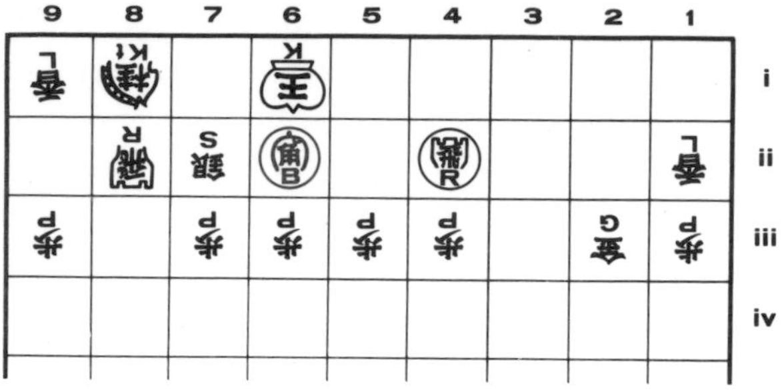

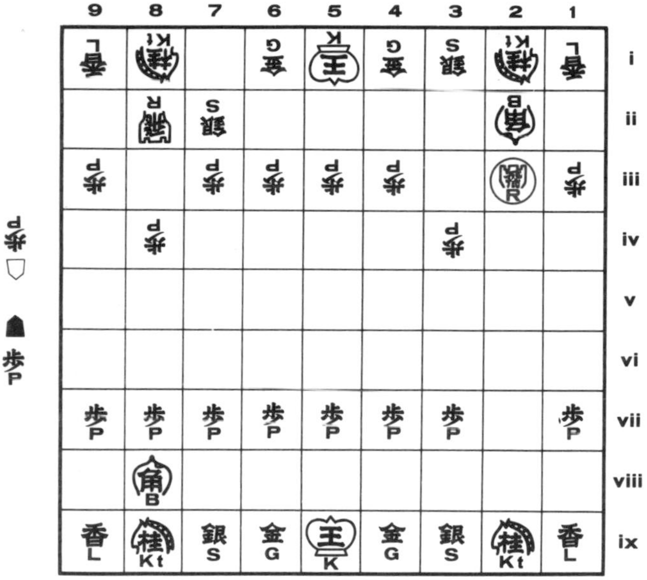

Before finishing with this little game, there are two points which it will help you to have explained. We go back to after his fourth move, namely 3 iv P.

Let us see what will happen if you make the most tempting move, promoting your Rook on 2 iii. You play:

5. 2 iii R (promotes) (diagram)

He replies:

. . . 3 ii G
attacking your promoted Rook.

Now if you retire to 2 viii (or anywhere else along the file) he simply drops his Pawn on 2 iii. You cannot take it because it is protected by his Gold.

Have a good look at this position. The only way you can attack his Pawn on 2 iii is to drop your Pawn on 2 iv. But when you do, he takes and you retake with your Rook. Then he drops the Pawn (just captured) onto 2 iii, and you have to move away again.

You can never break through now unless you bring up another piece. For instance you might use your Silver on 3 ix and send it plodding painfully up the file to help break through.

☖ 歩 P

☗ 歩 P 歩 P

9	8	7	6	5	4	3	2	1	
香 L	桂 Kt		金 G	王 K		銀 S	桂 Kt	香 L	i
	飛 R	銀 S				金 G	角 B		ii
歩 P		歩 P	歩 P	歩 P	歩 P			歩 P	iii
	歩 P					龍 R			iv
									v
									vi
歩 P	歩 P	歩 P	歩 P	歩 P	歩 P	歩 P		歩 P	vii
	角 B								viii
香 L	桂 Kt	銀 S	金 G	王 K	金 G	銀 S	桂 Kt	香 L	ix

Instead of retreating the promoted Rook when he attacks it with 3 ii G, you can try taking his Pawn on 3 iv (diagram). You now have two Pawns in hand. Furthermore you threaten to drop your Pawn on 2 iv and then promote it on 2 iii.

Your opponent however stops your plan by dropping his one Pawn onto 2 iii. This is an important principle of defense in Shogi—*When the opponent can make an effective drop on a vulnerable square, forestall him by dropping a piece there yourself.*

. . . 2 iii P drops

The situation is now similar to the last variation. You can only attack this Pawn by dropping your own Pawn onto 2 iv, and when you do he just takes.

True, you have now moved him off the square 2 iii, and you can drop your second Pawn there. But it is merely a drop and not a promotion. He quietly moves his Bishop out, to 4 iv or 5 v. If your Pawn advances, he will then take it—with the Bishop, not one of the other pieces.

All you have is a slight advantage, but there is no breakthrough and nothing like the quick win which you got in the game. You will have to bring up further pieces, and meantime he has a good chance of winning your Pawn on 2 iii, which is rather isolated.

	9	8	7	6	5	4	3	2	1
i	香 L	桂 Kt	銀 S	金 G	王 K		銀 S	桂 Kt	香 L
ii		飛 R					金 G	角 B	
iii	歩 P		歩 P	歩 P	歩 P	歩 P	歩 P	歩 P	歩 P
iv									
v		歩 P						歩 P	
vi									
vii	歩 P	歩 P	歩 P	歩 P	歩 P	歩 P	歩 P		歩 P
viii		角 B	金 G					飛 R	
ix	香 L	桂 Kt	銀 S		王 K	金 G	銀 S	桂 Kt	香 L

AN INTRODUCTION TO THE OPENINGS

THE great variety of openings in Shogi can be divided into two groups:

(1) *Static Rook openings,* where the Rook remains on his original file and operates from there for at least some time;

(2) *Ranging Rook openings,* where the Rook leaves his file and moves to one of the centre files or even to the other side of the board.

I. The Static Rook Openings

The static Rook openings are easier to handle. They in turn can be divided into a "safe" line where the Bishops are not exchanged and a "wild" line where the Bishops are (or can be) exchanged.

We shall look first at a safe, orthodox position in the early stages. Both sides have advanced the Pawn in front of the Rook two squares, and then both have protected the danger point by reinforcing it with a Gold (diagram).

In this line the opener generally makes the two moves with his Pawn and then moves his Gold to 7 viii. One might think that with the advantage of the move, the opener could omit the Gold move and go on to play his Pawn to 2 iv and "get in first," but for tactical reasons too complicated to explain here, this is not so. He must protect his square at 8 vii, even though he gives his opponent the chance to do the same on the other side.

A simple line now is:

	Black	White
4.	2 iv P	Same P
5.	Same R	2 iii P drops
6.	2 viii R	8 vi P
7.	Same P	Same R
8.	8 vii P drops	8 ii R

Now we have a symmetrical position. Each of you has a clear line in front of his Rook right up to the enemy bastions, and each of you has a Pawn in hand. At the moment you have each only one file on which you can use it (see rule, page 41), but later, if you sacrifice a Pawn on some other file, this Pawn in hand may be dropped with decisive effect.

9	8	7	6	5	4	3	2	1	
L	Kt	S	G	K		S	Kt	L	i
	R					G	B		ii
P		P	P	P	P	P	P	P	iii
									iv
									v
									vi
P	P	P	P	P	P	P		P	vii
	B	G				S	R		viii
L	Kt	S		K	G		Kt	L	ix

9. 3 viii S (diagram)

We give you a separate diagram, as this is the characteristic move of an important opening called *Bo-gin*. Literally it means "Pole-silver," and the point is that Black intends to send his Silver climbing up file 2, like a pole so to speak, in order to help to break through at the other end.

It will take several moves, however, and meanwhile White prepares his own formation.

		. . . 3 iv P
10.	2 vii S	. . . 4 ii S (sometimes White plays 3 iii B here instead)
11.	2 vi S	. . . 3 iii S
12.	2 v S	

	9	8	7	6	5	4	3	2	1	
	香 L	桂 Kt	銀 S	金 G	王 K			桂 Kt	香 L	i
		飛 R					金 G	角 B		ii
	歩 P		歩 P	歩 P	歩 P	歩 P	銀 S	歩 P	歩 P	iii
歩 P ☖							歩 P			iv
								銀 S		v
☗ 歩 P										vi
	歩 P	歩 P	歩 P	歩 P	歩 P	歩 P	歩 P		歩 P	vii
		角 B	金 G					飛 R		viii
	香 L	桂 Kt	銀 S		王 K	金 G		桂 Kt	香 L	ix

In the diagramed position, the opponent has met the Bo-gin attack correctly, and there is no chance of a quick win. Sometimes you can break through by advancing the Pawn in front of your Lance, 1 vi, 1 v, 1 iv, and then exchanging off both Lances, remaining with your Silver on 1 iv. Then you get in on 2 iii. But this is a beginner's maneuver at this stage. If your opponent meets it properly by playing 1 iv P as soon as you play 1 vi P, you can do nothing further. It is mentioned here because frequently in the Shogi openings you will find that when one player advances the Lance Pawn, the other one immediately follows suit. The idea is to rule out this kind of attack from the beginning.

If you go on with your "attack" and play 2 iv P drops, your opponent takes and then you exchange the Silvers. He plays 2 iii P drops and your Rook is driven away. You have gained nothing because you each have a Silver in hand, but you have wasted all the moves it took you to get your Silver to 2 iv. Your opponent has opened his Bishop's diagonal and stands better.

Note in this line that you cannot unthinkingly take the Pawn on 3 iv, because your opponent has the unpleasant possibility of dropping his Silver from hand onto 2 viii—then unprotected by your Rook. From there he could gobble up your Knight or Lance or even both. He might not think it worth doing, but it is a possibility that must always be watched when you take your Rook off its main file.

So you must develop your game systematically and slowly.

12.		. . . 5 ii G
13.	7 vi P	. . . 4 iv P

9	8	7	6	5	4	3	2	1	
L	Kt	S		K			Kt	L	i
	R			G		G	B		ii
P		P	P	P		S	P	P	iii
					P	P			iv
							S		v
		P							vi
P	P		P	P	P	P		P	vii
	B	G					R		viii
L	Kt	S		K	G		Kt	L	ix

☖ P　☗ P

This is where we pass into deeper opening theory. Your immediate naïve attack has been brought to a halt; by playing 7 vi P you opened the line of your Bishop and created some vague possibilities of sacrificing this Bishop at some time for the defending Silver. But your opponent put an end to all these ideas by playing 4 iv P.

You can still of course exchange off the Silvers by playing 2 iv P drops. But if you look round you will see that there's nowhere in his camp where you could drop a Silver with advantage.

To get an attack going, you will have to loosen things up considerably, push forward some Pawns, and try to get your Knight on 2 ix ultimately into the fray.

Probably you feel you would like to try these things right away. Here it is that the experience of Shogi masters of the past comes in. Their experience is that if you go for a big attack, with the consequent loosening of the position on both sides, without first bringing your King into absolute safety, then you come off badly in the end.

As a beginner looking at the position, it seems that your King *is* in safety. He has a Gold next to him and another pair on the left only one square away. But that is not nearly enough. There are far too many loose squares round him. Look at those two unprotected Pawns right in front of him! Later on, there will be no time to defend them.

Now everyone is told this when he begins to play Shogi, and almost everyone forgets it. You will have some bitter experiences before you come to realize the importance of getting your King to a well-fortified "castle" before you loosen up the game.

Just for your information, I am going to give the sort of thing that might happen if you went on with your attack—advancing and exchanging several pieces, leaving the King as he is now (diagram).

☖ 歩 P, 桂 Kt, 銀 S

	9	8	7	6	5	4	3	2	1	
	香 L	桂 Kt	銀 S						香 L	i
		飛 R				角 B	金 G	王 K		ii
	歩 P		歩 P	歩 P	歩 P	金 G		歩 P	歩 P	iii
						歩 P	歩 P			iv
						歩 P				v
			歩 P				歩 P		桂 Kt	vi
	歩 P	歩 P		歩 P	歩 P				歩 P	vii
		角 B	金 G					飛 R		viii
	香 L	桂 Kt	銀 S		王 K	金 G			香 L	ix

☗ 銀 S, 歩 P

You seem to have quite a nice attack going: you have just dropped your Knight on 1 vi, with the idea of next dropping the Pawn on 2 iv and retaking with the Knight when he captures.

Alas, he comes in with a strong check by 1 v B. If you move away, he plays 3 vii B (promotes) and chases your Rook. So you interpose 4 viii S drops. Now he drops 3 vii S. In desperation you can try your other threat and play 4 iv P, but he easily parries by quietly moving 3 iii G (from 4 iii). Notice how snug his King is compared with yours.

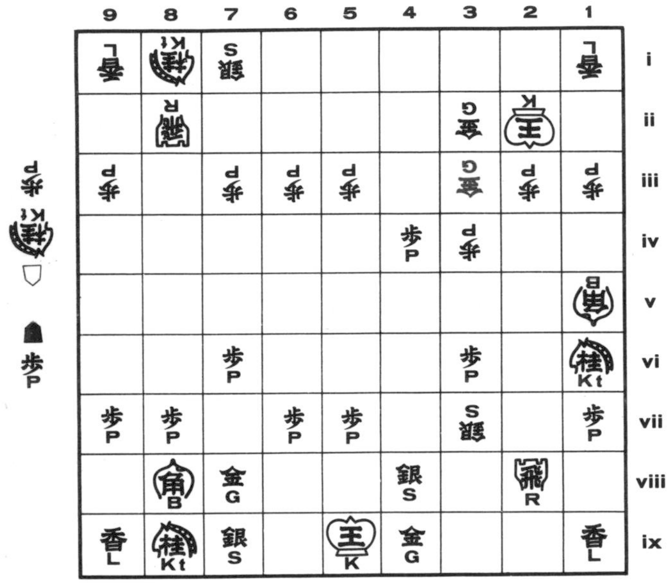

Suppose to save your Rook you play:

2 v R

Then he knocks out everything round your King in two moves—

. . . 4 viii S

Same G

. . . Same B (promotes)

Same K

Now your King is quite bare of defenders and surrounded with open lines. Your game will soon collapse.

If you find this hard to believe, experiment in different ways till you find out how to attack in such cases. Begin for instance by dropping (as an attacking piece, of course—you have now changed sides) 4 vi S.

But the main point was for you to see how quickly the King became absolutely bare and open, when he began from an even slightly loose position.

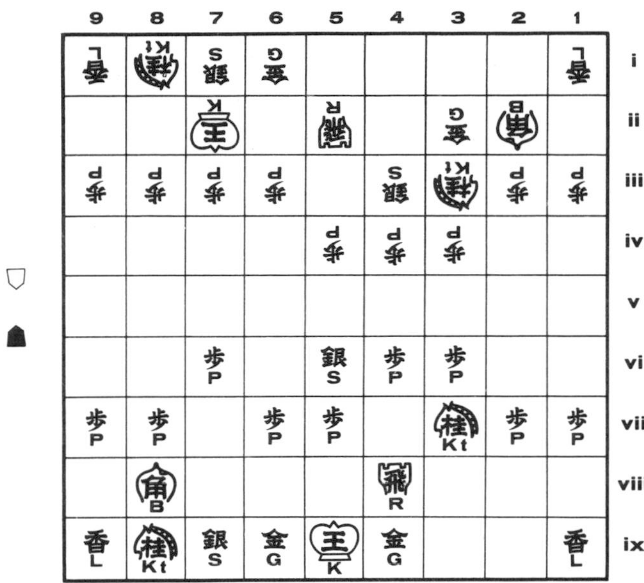

A little bit more about this crucial point. This is a different kind of opening. You have moved your Rook to the fourth file to operate there. But the thing is that while you have been building up your attacking position, your adversary has begun to move his King out of the way. He hasn't finished castling yet, but anyway he is out of any direct lines of attack. You have been content to leave your King in the middle. No doubt it looks secure enough, but see what happens the moment the attack gets underway and pieces are exchanged.

	BLACK	WHITE
1.	4 v P	. . . Same P
2.	Same Kt	. . . Same Kt
3.	2 ii B (promotes)	

It makes no difference whether you exchange Bishops here or let your opponent do it.

. . . Same G

4. 4 v S

Your position looks comfortable enough. You are about to drop a Pawn on 4 iv, and then take his Pawn on the third file, and then with that support you can promote your Pawn into a Gold—which should decide the game.

But you have overlooked one thing—the Bishops are exchanged and are "wild." You have nowhere very useful to put yours, but he can make a hammer-blow with his. He plays:

. . . 3 vii B drops (diagram)

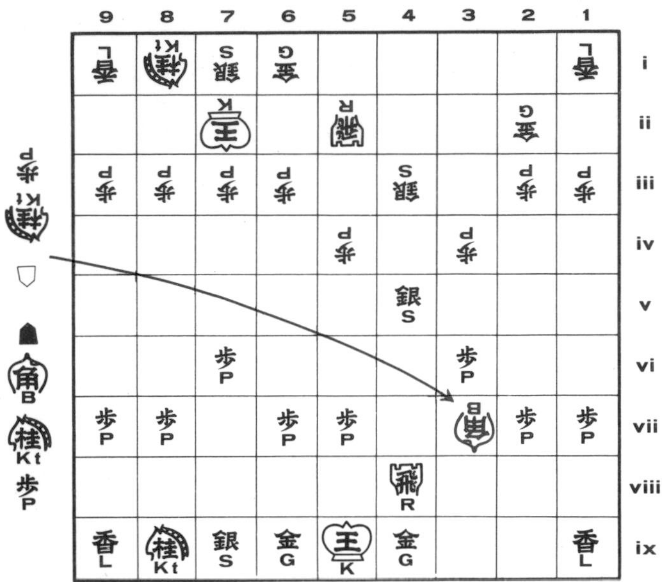

Now the slaughter is on. He threatens not merely to win your Rook for his Bishop, but to win it for a Pawn—by dropping his Pawn on 4 vii. You can try to prevent this.

6. 5 viii G (from 6 ix) . . . 5 v Kt drops threatening the same thing again.

7. 3 viii G

This move is made to end the threats once and for all. There are other moves, but they all end up badly. He now takes your Rook to use on the open lines.

. . . 4 viii B (promotes)

What happens next depends on how you take this. If you take with the King, it is one disaster; if with one of the Golds, it is another.

This position is given a separate diagram only to help you to realize just how exposed the King is in the center. Have a look at the variations.

If you take the promoted Bishop with your King, he could of course drop the Rook (which he has just captured from you) onto 4 vi, and in his next move take your unprotected Silver on 4 v.

But stronger would be first to drop his Pawn on 4 vii, giving check, and then—depending which side you went with your King—he would drop his Rook on the last rank, giving check and then capturing either the Silver or Lance. If you came up with your King to 3 vii, he would drop the Rook on 4 ix, attacking the same pieces.

If you took the Bishop with either Gold, he could still drop his Rook

	9	8	7	6	5	4	3	2	1	
	L	Kt	S	G					L	i
			K		R			G		ii
P	P	P	P	P		S		P	P	iii
R					P		P			iv
					Kt	S				v
			P				P			vi
B	P	P		P	P			P	P	vii
Kt P					G	B	G			viii
	L	Kt	S		K				L	ix

on 2 ix, capturing the Lance and promoting next move after you moved away from the check or interposed.

Lastly, if you captured with the Gold on 5 vii, he could play his Knight to 6 vii and not promote. This would mean he would check you and at the same time attack the Silver on 7 ix, which he would win for a Knight.

This example may have convinced you how energetically a King in the center can be attacked. In both the cases we have given, the decisive blow was given by a Bishop. This is the most frequent case. When attacks get going, the Bishops often get exchanged, and the man who does not have his King properly guarded finds himself in trouble. Of course you can try to avoid exchanging the Bishops, but then it has a cramping effect on your whole game, because you so often need to have a Bishop yourself to get on with your own attack.

Now we go back briefly to the Bo-gin variation to see how the two sides get their Kings to safety.

We have gone back to the position in the Bo-gin opening, and you will now understand the next move assigned to you.

14. 6 ix K

This is the first of a series of moves to take your King to safety off the open lines.

		. . . 4 iii G (from 5 ii)
15.	6 viii S	. . . 6 ii S

▽ 歩 P　　▲ 歩 P

	9	8	7	6	5	4	3	2	1	
	香 L	桂 Kt	銀 S		王 K			桂 Kt	香 L	i
		飛 R			金 G		金 G	角 B		ii
	歩 P		歩 P	歩 P	歩 P		銀 S	歩 P	歩 P	iii
						歩 P	歩 P			iv
								銀 S		v
			歩 P							vi
	歩 P	歩 P		歩 P	歩 P	歩 P	歩 P		歩 P	vii
		角 B	金 G					飛 R		viii
	香 L	桂 Kt	銀 S		王 K	金 G		桂 Kt	香 L	ix

16. 5 viii G . . . 5 iv P
17. 4 vi P . . . 4 i K

Having put your King to left of center, with three guardsmen in front of him, you begin to prepare your attack. You opponent is still getting his King to the side—he has prepared a group of three men, two Golds and a Silver, and ultimately he will shelter his King somewhere behind them. Quite often he will bring the Bishop to 3 i and then to 4 ii, and the King slowly moves round to 2 ii. All this has to be properly timed.

However in order to show off the Bo-gin attack, we illustrate a line in which the opponent neglects to get his King to safety but tries to initiate a counter-attack on the other wing.

We give a few more moves without much explanation, because to go into many variations is profitless at this stage. What you have to do is to get a general idea of the sort of possibilities to look out for. From the diagram:

18. 3 vi P . . . 6 iv P
19. 3 vii Kt . . . 7 iv P
20. 5 vi P . . . 6 iii S
21. 4 v P

This is the crucial move of the attack.

You have four active pieces, the Rook, the Silver on 2 v, the Knight

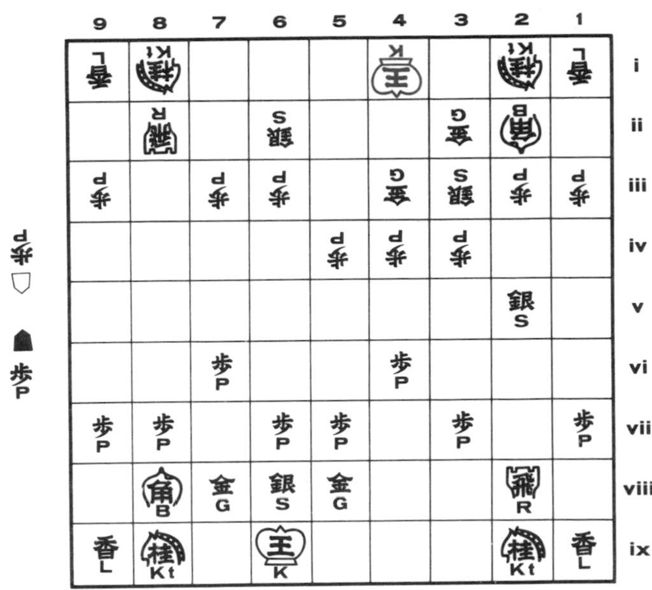

on 3 vii, and (very important) the Bishop on the long diagonal. First we assume that the opponent takes this Pawn.

		. . . Same P
22.	Same Kt	. . . 4 iv S

At first glance at the diagram, your opponent's position does not look too bad. He is threatening your Knight, and it would seem that you must support it with a Pawn. Then he can advance his Pawn to 3 v, and if you take, he recaptures with his Silver, finally breaking into your position.

If you do not take, you must withdraw your Silver when he takes your Pawn.

However the key to this position is that White has had to move his Silver on 3 iii, which is *the key to his defense.* You cheerfully let your Knight go for the sake of the breakthrough with your Silver and Rook.

23. 2 iv P drops . . . 4 v S

Your opponent takes the Knight, and in so doing opens the line for exchange of Bishops.

24. 2 ii B (promotes) . . . Same G

25. 2 iii P (promotes)

Now you see the advantage of having moved your King to safety! If your King were on 5 ix, its original square, White could make a devastating check with the exchanged Bishop on 3 vii. As it is, he cannot use his Bishop in hand very effectively. His King, on the other hand, is exposed.

. . . Same G

26. 1 iv S

with a very strong attack.

Let us finally study this attacking formation going into action (diagram). Notice, by the way, that it would have been a mistake to play the Silver to 2 iv instead of 1 iv. White would have replied 4 vi B drops, forking Rook and Silver and capturing the Silver for nothing on the next move.

Black is about to promote his Rook. With White's exposed King, the Rook will exercise strong threats.

Black's second threat, no less important, is to play:

4 iv P drops.

It looks as if White can simply take this with his Gold, but if he does, Black drops his Bishop from hand onto the key-square 7 i, forking the Rook and the Gold. This fork with the Bishop occurs very frequently. If White plays 4 ii R to protect the Gold, Black promotes his Bishop on 5 iii, attacking the Rook, the Gold, and also the loose Silver on 6 iii. White will very soon collapse.

In the diagramed position, White's comparatively best defense

	9	8	7	6	5	4	3	2	1	
	L	Kt				K		Kt	L	i
		R								ii
	P			S		G		G	P	iii
			P	P	P		P		S	iv
						S				v
			P		P		P			vi
	P	P		P					P	vii
			G	S	G			R		viii
	L	Kt		K					L	ix

☖ B Kt P P P

☗ B P P

would be to drop a Pawn on 2 ii, and when Black captures the Gold on 2 iii, not to recapture. Instead he might try a direct counter-attack by dropping his Bishop on 4 vi. When Black moves the Rook say to 2 ix, White promotes the Bishop on 3 vii and tries to get up something by dropping his Knight on 4 vi.

If Black drops his Pawn on 4 iv, White just moves his Gold back to 4 ii. Black will have to play carefully, say by shifting his King to 7 ix and retreating his Gold to 5 ix when White drops the Knight. But Black should ultimately win.

A good way to meet the Bo-gin attack is to use the Bishop on 3 iii and bring up the defending Silver by way of 2 ii. We give here one standard variation, ending with the diagram, in which White stands satisfactorily. If Black attempts to rush the attack here or previously, he generally comes to grief.

Go back to the position on page 62, in which Black has just made the typical Bo-gin move—3 viii S.

		. . . 3 iv P
2.	2 vii S	. . . 3 iii B
3.	3 vi S	

(Experts often elect to climb the "pole" via 3 vi; it gives an additional option of going to the center as a surprise.)

		. . . 2 ii S
4.	6 ix K	. . . 4 i K
5.	5 viii G	. . . 8 iv R

☖ 歩 P　☗ 歩 P

	9	8	7	6	5	4	3	2	1	
	香 L	桂 Kt				王 K		桂 Kt	香 L	i
				銀 S	金 G		金 G	銀 S		ii
			歩 P	歩 P	歩 P	歩 P	角 B	歩 P		iii
	歩 P	飛 R					歩 P		歩 P	iv
						銀 S				v
	歩 P		歩 P			歩 P			歩 P	vi
		歩 P		歩 P	歩 P		歩 P			vii
		角 B	金 G		金 G			飛 R		viii
	香 L	桂 Kt	銀 S	王 K				桂 Kt	香 L	ix

This is an important move in the defense. If at an earlier stage, say on move 4, instead of shifting his King, Black plays 2 v S, then White immediately plays his Rook up to 8 iv, forestalling and blocking the attack. White then generally has difficulties with his game.

6. 4 vi P . . . 6 ii S
7. 7 vi P . . . 9 iv P
8. 1 vi P . . . 1 iv P
9. 9 vi P

These Pawn moves on the sides are to threaten and neutralize attacks with the Pawn and Lance. They occur in many openings and have to be made sooner or later.

. . . 5 ii G

10. 4 v S

Black springs a slight surprise by attacking with his Silver on 4 v instead of 2 v (diagram).

Here a "book" line directs White to play 7 iv P, and when Black takes the Pawn on 3 iv, White advances 7 v P after exchanging the Bishops. Black protects the hanging Silver with his Bishop, dropping on 5 vi. Then White plays 2 iv P, aiming at an ultimate exchange of Rooks. If he can secure this, he does well, because he can drop the captured Rook effectively on 4 ix and clean up.

There is absolutely no point in trying to burden you with a lot of opening variations. Until you have played quite a lot of Shogi, they

	9	8	7	6	5	4	3	2	1	
	香 L	桂 Kt	銀 S	金 G	王 K	金 G	銀 S	桂 Kt	香 L	i
		飛 R						角 B		ii
	歩 P		歩 P	歩 P	歩 P	歩 P		歩 P	歩 P	iii
							歩 P			iv
☖		歩 P						歩 P		v
☗			歩 P							vi
	歩 P	歩 P		歩 P	歩 P	歩 P	歩 P		歩 P	vii
		角 B						飛 R		viii
	香 L	桂 Kt	銀 S	金 G	王 K	金 G	銀 S	桂 Kt	香 L	ix

will be no use to you because the "book" lines deal only with the strongest defenses. If you know those by heart, you will still be baffled when your opponent makes an inferior move, because you have not enough Shogi experience to refute it.

In these opening lines we are just showing you the kind of thing that can happen, so that you can watch out for the chances on both sides.

Still dealing with the static Rook openings, it makes a great difference if you both open the Bishop line early. That means an exchange of Bishops can take place any time. When the Bishops are in hand, you have to be very careful not to leave loose pieces lying about; you have to watch particularly for the Bishop check. It is more important than ever to get your King stowed safely away from any open lines.

Notice in the diagram that you have played 7 vi P and he has played 3 iv P, which means the Bishops are confronting each other along an open line. Suppose you go on happily as before, advancing the Pawn in front of your Rook in order to exchange it off and get a Pawn in hand. You at once enter a forest of complications.

From the position in the previous diagram, you played 2 iv P; he took it and you retook.

Your opponent immediately exchanged Bishops and dropped his captured Bishop in hand on to the key-square 3 iii, forking your Rook and the loose unprotected Silver on 8 viii (diagram).

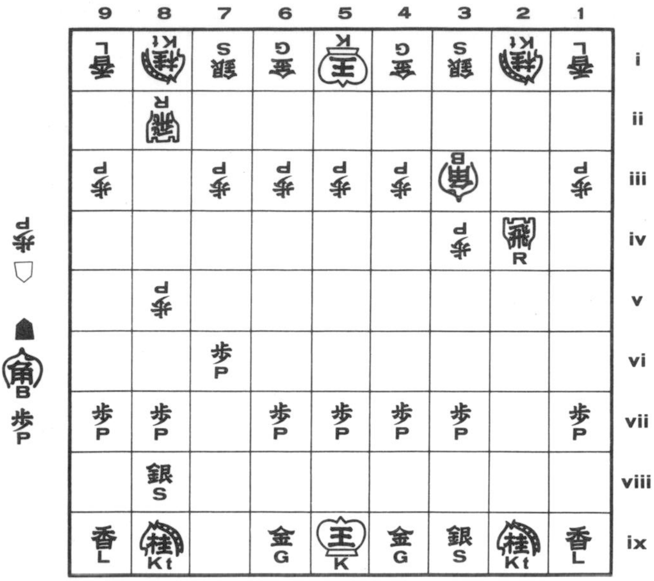

9	8	7	6	5	4	3	2	1	
香 L	桂 Kt	銀 S	金 G	王 K	金 G	銀 S	桂 Kt	香 L	i
	飛 R								ii
歩 P		歩 P	歩 P	歩 P	歩 P	角 B		歩 P	iii
						歩 P	飛 R		iv
	歩 P								v
		歩 P							vi
歩 P	歩 P		歩 P	歩 P	歩 P	歩 P		歩 P	vii
	銀 S								viii
香 L	桂 Kt		金 G	王 K	金 G	銀 S	桂 Kt	香 L	ix

☖ 歩 P

☗ 角 B 歩 P

Have a good look at this position—it is typical. The pieces on both sides are mostly in their original positions, and weakly defended. But you are the worse off.

You can capture the Knight and promote your Rook, but meanwhile he captures the Silver, promoting his Bishop. There are various ingenious little tricks you can try by dropping your own Bishop from hand, for instance onto 7 vii. But he takes your Knight on 8 ix, and experience show that his Silver and Gold are able to keep off your attempts to attack his King, while he can mount an effective one against your King.

It is quite good practice to take a position like this one and experiment with it for yourself. Perhaps—who knows?—you will find a satisfactory variation for Black that has been overlooked. But probably you will conclude that you must reluctantly bring your Rook back straight to 2 viii, to protect the Silver on 8 ii.

Now your opponent plays:

. . . 2 vi P drops

This is much stronger than the superficially attractive 2 vii P drop. It threatens to make a Gold, whereas from 2 vii it can achieve nothing when the Rook quietly moves away.

In the diagramed position you cannot take the Pawn because then your Silver would go. So you interpose your Knight between the attacking Bishop and your Silver.

	9	8	7	6	5	4	3	2	1	
	香 L	桂 Kt	銀 S	金 G	王 K	金 G	銀 S	桂 Kt	香 L	i
		飛 R								ii
	歩 P		歩 P	歩 P	歩 P	歩 P	角 B		歩 P	iii
							歩 P			iv
		歩 P								v
			歩 P					歩 P		vi
	歩 P	歩 P		歩 P	歩 P	歩 P	歩 P		歩 P	vii
		銀 S						飛 R		viii
	香 L	桂 Kt		金 G	王 K	金 G	銀 S	桂 Kt	香 L	ix

☖

☗ 角 B 歩 P

1. 7 vii Kt

You now threaten to take the Pawn. However he has a strong move which protects it and at the same time prepares to advance and promote it.

. . . 2 ii R

2. 3 viii S

This holds everything for the moment, but White still can apply some pressure. He could even try a sacrifice by :

. . . 7 vii B, though this is a dubious line.

Probably his best is to get his pieces into some sort of formation first and keep the option of the various possibilities. Note that you dare not exchange off anything much—for instance to give him a Silver in hand would be to invite him to make the drop 2 vii S (which would finish you off out of hand!).

Many players (including a good many of the leading experts) block the Bishop lines early by putting a piece, sometimes a Pawn, in between. Often it is a Silver on 7 vii or 3 iii, or both.

When this happens, the Bishop lines only get opened when the big attack takes place and the battlefield clears. It is then, however, frequently the decisive factor—the one who can get an effective Bishop drop wins the game.

You must take care, when interposing a Silver, that the opponent

	9	8	7	6	5	4	3	2	1	
	香 L	桂 Kt	銀 S	金 G	王 K		銀 S	桂 Kt	香 L	i
		飛 R					金 G	角 B		ii
	歩 P		歩 P	歩 P	歩 P	歩 P		歩 P	歩 P	iii
							歩 P			iv
☖		歩 P								v
☗			歩 P					歩 P		vi
	歩 P	歩 P	銀 S	歩 P	歩 P	歩 P	歩 P		歩 P	vii
		角 B				銀 S		飛 R		viii
	香 L	桂 Kt		金 G	王 K	金 G		桂 Kt	香 L	ix

cannot make a sacrifice. He can only do so as a rule in the very opening stages, but the diagramed position is one that frequently arises between beginners.

Many novices do not realize that the sacrifice will be a winning line, and so do not make it.

In this opening the moves were:

7 vi P	. . . 8 iv P
6 viii S	. . . 3 iv P
7 vii S	. . . 8 v P
2 vi P	. . . 3 ii G
4 viii S (diagram)	

This is the losing move; it breaks the connection between the Rook and the Bishop, which becomes momentarily undefended. 7 viii G was the right move in this and all similar positions.

	. . . 8 vi P
Same P	. . . Same R

This is a fine move which will win. He gives up the Rook but will win your Bishop, promoting his own. You have almost nowhere to drop your captured Rook, whereas his promoted Bishop will massacre your minor pieces. With these and the Bishop in hand, he will win easily.

There are other variations earlier, but White plays boldly and breaks up Black's position always.

	9	8	7	6	5	4	3	2	1	
	香 L	桂 Kt						桂 Kt	香 L	i
		飛 R		銀 S		角 B	金 G	王 K		ii
	歩 P		歩 P	歩 P		金 G	銀 S	歩 P	歩 P	iii
					歩 P	歩 P	歩 P			iv
		歩 P						歩 P		v
			歩 P	歩 P	歩 P					vi
	歩 P	歩 P	銀 S	金 G		歩 P	歩 P		歩 P	vii
		王 K	金 G	角 B		銀 S		飛 R		viii
	香 L	桂 Kt						桂 Kt	香 L	ix

II. The Yagura Opening

Here is a longish series of moves leading to the *yagura* position shown in the diagram. It is one of the strongest and safest in Shogi. The only trouble is that your opponent can adopt it equally, and then it is not easy to get a decisive advantage.

7 vi P	. . . 8 iv P
6 viii S	. . . 3 iv P
7 vii S	. . . 8 v P
2 vi P	. . . 3 ii G
7 viii G	. . . 4 ii S
4 viii S	. . . 6 ii S
2 v P	. . . 3 iii S
5 vi P	. . . 5 iv P
5 viii G	. . . 5 ii G
6 vi P	. . . 4 iv P
6 vii G (from 5 viii)	. . . 4 iii G (from 5 ii)
7 ix B	. . . 3 i B
6 viii B	. . . 4 ii B
6 ix K	. . . 4 i K
7 ix K	. . . 3 i K
8 viii K	. . . 2 ii K (diagram)

Both sides are well entrenched and have mobilized their forces. One side must now risk the attack; in so doing he will have to loosen his position, and in the general exchanges which follow, the attacker's side will, as a rule, have more "holes" where pieces from his opponent's hand can drop. This means that if the attack does not come off, the counter-attack often wins the day.

Black here will probably cautiously work his Silver forward behind the Pawn on the third file, exchanging the latter if necessary. If he gets his Silver say to 3 vi, he can bring up the Knight behind it and finally try the thrust 4 v P. If he plays properly he can force White to take this Pawn, and then the Knight comes into the game. When the Knight comes forward like this, Black must have all his pieces in the best positions for the breakthrough. There is no time afterwards because the Knight gets lost immediately if White just has time to drop a Pawn in front of it.

These are just a few hints for middle-game strategy; actual play is needed before you can absorb more.

III. The Ranging Rook Openings

In this series of openings (and many of them transpose into each other) the King is castled into safety to the *right,* after bringing the Rook across from his usual station. The Rook can be brought to:

(1) the center file—*Naka-bisha,* or centered Rook formation, which often leads to a fierce attack backed by the Rook, though if the attack is made too soon and does not come off, the position is ruined;

(2) confront the other Rook—to make a *Mukai-bisha,* or facing Rook, which is a tough defensive game, waiting for the chance to counter-attack;

(3) the two intermediate files (between the center and the facing Rook position).

However, the Rook is not planted on one file and left there. In the ranging Rook openings he shifts from file to file as occasion warrants, and must be handled very flexibly. In the static Rook openings, on the contrary, the Rook sometimes spends the whole game on his original square, exercising pressure from there but never moving.

A typical Ranging Rook opening might begin with these moves:

7 vi P	. . . 3 iv P
6 vi P	

You do this, deliberately blocking the line of the Bishops. This move is very often played by one or both sides. The idea is to obtain the desired formation without being harassed by constant tactical threats from Bishops in hand.

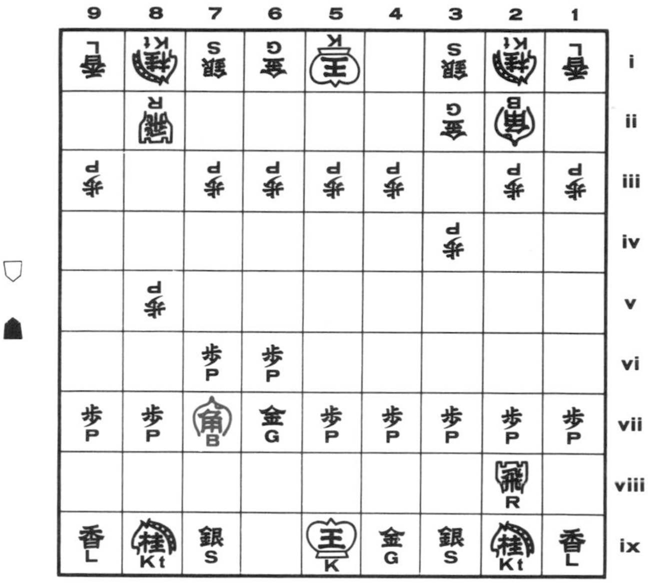

. . . 8 iv P

The opponent is playing a static Rook.

7 viii G	. . . 3 ii G
6 vii G	. . . 8 v P
7 vii B (diagram)	

It is essential to play this move the moment White threatens 8 vi P. The breakthrough is to be checked by the Bishop, now and for a long time to come.

The Rook will be brought to 8 viii, 7 viii, 6 viii, or 5 viii, and the King will be tucked away on 2 viii, protected by at least two guardsmen, and preferably three.

We give a few more moves—the opponent goes into a secure yagura position.

	. . . 4 ii S
7 viii R	. . . 4 iv P
4 viii K	. . . 5 ii G
3 viii K	. . . 4 i K
2 viii K	. . . 3 iii S
3 viii S	

This is a very important move, characteristic of the castling formation in the ranging Rook openings. The Gold and Silver mutually protect each other. Later on, if the Rooks have been exchanged (as they often are in the ranging Rook variations), the

9	8	7	6	5	4	3	2	1	
L	Kt	S					Kt	L	i
	R					G	K		ii
P			P	B	G	S	P	P	iii
		P		P	P	P			iv
	P								v
		P	P	P	P				vi
P	P	B	G		S	P	P	P	vii
	R					S	K		viii
L	Kt				G		Kt	L	ix

enemy will drop a Rook say on 6 ix. Experience shows that this formation gives the strongest resistance.

. . . 4 iii G (from 5 ii)

6 viii S — . . . 3 i B

This Bishop is to be used as an attacking piece on other diatonals.

5 vi P — . . . 5 iv P

8 viii R

The enemy threatened a breakthrough with 8 vi P, supported now not only by the Rook but also by the Bishop from 3 i. You have neutralized the threat—this is an example of how the Rook is used in these openings.

. . . 5 iii B

5 vii S — . . . 3 i K

4 vi P — . . . 2 ii K

4 viii S

This move was developed by Master Ohno, a great authority on these openings. The Silver is to go to 4 vii.

. . . 7 iv P

4 vii S (diagram)

We leave the opening here. Black will finally play 3 vi P and bring his Knight out. Then with 4 v P he can develop some threats. White can hamper him by bringing his Bishop to 7 iii.

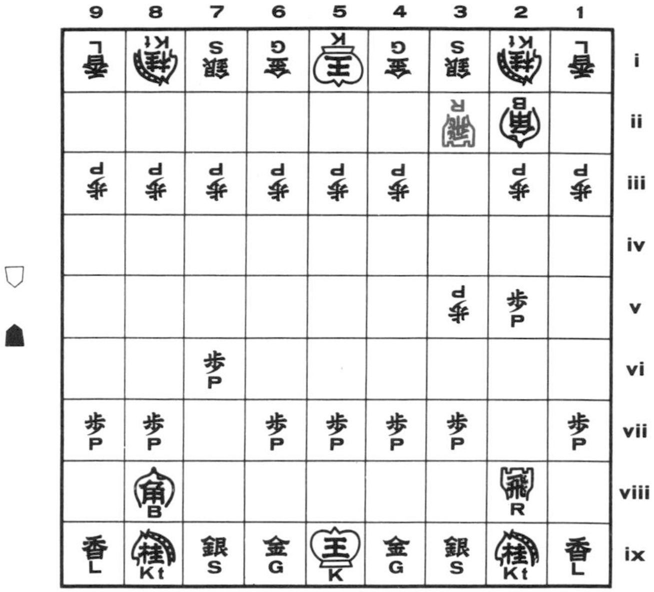

	9	8	7	6	5	4	3	2	1	
	香 L	桂 Kt	銀 S	金 G	王 K	金 G	銀 S	桂 Kt	香 L	i
							飛 R	角 B		ii
	歩 P	歩 P	歩 P	歩 P	歩 P	歩 P		歩 P	歩 P	iii
										iv
							歩 P	歩 P		v
			歩 P							vi
	歩 P	歩 P		歩 P	歩 P	歩 P	歩 P		歩 P	vii
		角 B						飛 R		viii
	香 L	桂 Kt	銀 S	金 G	王 K	金 G	銀 S	桂 Kt	香 L	ix

The Ishida Variation

This is one of the ranging Rook lines which can bowl you over very easily if you have never seen it before, and in just a few moves. It is said to have been invented over a century ago by a blind chess master named Ishida.

This time we shall put you on the receiving end.

7 vi P	. . . 3 iv P
2 vi P	. . . 3 v P
2 v P	. . . 3 ii R (diagram)

These are the distinctive moves of the variation.

If you play here mechanically 2 iv P, he takes it and you retake with your Rook. Now he plays 3 vi P, a keymove of many of his attacking lines.

(1) If you do nothing, he takes your Pawn, promoting his to Gold, protected by his Rook.

(2) If you try to defend with 4 viii S, he exchanges Bishops and plays 3 iii B drops, attacking your Rook and the loose Silver on 8 viii. We have seen before that this line generally loses for you (page 76), and it does here.

(3) If you retire your Rook, he takes the Pawn, exchanges Bishops, and begins to worry you with Bishop drops on 5 v or even 1 v in some cases.

(4) If you take his Pawn on 3 vi, he exchanges Bishops and forks your Rook and King by dropping on 1 v.

The best lines are: instead of 2 iv P, you play 4 viii S. You have to be careful, but you should survive. Instead of 2 iv P, you exchange the Bishops and then quietly play 8 viii S. If you keep your head, the opponent will eventually run out of moves.

	9	8	7	6	5	4	3	2	1	
	香 L							桂 Kt	香 L	i
		飛 R					金 G	王 K		ii
歩 P			桂 Kt	銀 S		金 G	銀 S	歩 P		iii
角 B	歩 P		歩 P	歩 P	歩 P	歩 P	歩 P		歩 P	iv
					歩 P			歩 P		v
角 B	歩 P	歩 P	歩 P	歩 P		銀 S	歩 P		歩 P	vi
		銀 S	桂 Kt	金 G		歩 P				vii
		王 K	金 G					飛 R		viii
	香 L							桂 Kt	香 L	ix

A FEW GAME POSITIONS

Position One

BY THE time you get this far, you should have played a number of games and have tried out some of the openings.

At first, if you are both beginners, one side will make a blunder which lets the other army in. But as you get mutual experience and learn how to organize your pieces (especially as you learn the proper way of castling your King), it will become increasingly difficult to see how to break open the position.

Now look at the diagram. You each have a Bishop in hand, but both sides seem fairly securely protected.

The key to the position is to notice that your opponent has two loose unprotected pieces: the Knight on 7 iii and the Silver on 6 iii. But if you just attacked by dropping your Bishop say on 4 i, he would move the Silver back to 5 ii, and you would lose your Bishop for a Silver. You have to find some way of combining your threat with a strong threat somewhere else.

With this in mind, play through the following moves:

3 v P	. . . Same P
Same S	. . . 3 iv P drop
2 iv P	

This is the first crucial move. You offer to sacrifice your Silver on

3 v in order to get a breakthrough. If he refuses the sacrifice and plays . . . Same P, then you do not retake at once but play 5 i B, threatening his loose Knight—and (next move) the Silver. When he protects the Knight, you exchange the Silvers on 2 iv and finally retake with the promoted Bishop. With this promoted Bishop to penetrate the enemy camp, you will win material and the game.

Play the variation over once or twice to convince yourself that it is so; he can do nothing with his Bishop and Silver in hand.

An expert might even win by direct attack, dropping a Pawn on 2 iii after the opponent takes the Pawn on 2 iv, then dropping the Bishop on 4 i, but it would be a risky line.

	9	8	7	6	5	4	3	2	1
i	香 L							桂 Kt	香 L
ii		飛 R					金 G	王 K	
iii			桂 Kt	銀 S		金 G	銀 S	歩 P	
iv	歩 P		歩 P	歩 P	歩 P	歩 P	歩 P	歩 P	歩 P
v					歩 P		銀 S		
vi	歩 P	歩 P	歩 P	歩 P					歩 P
vii		銀 S	桂 Kt	金 G		歩 P			
viii		王 K	金 G					飛 R	
ix	香 L							桂 Kt	香 L

☖ 角 B 歩 P

☗ 角 B 歩 P

Suppose that your opponent were to take the Silver which is going free on 3 v (diagram).

Your order of moves would be to play the Bishop to 4 i by dropping it from hand. Now you threaten his Silver on 6 iii, promoting your Bishop and soon afterwards capturing his Knight and then running the center Pawn through.

Imagine he protects his Silver, for instance by dropping his newly captured Silver from hand onto 5 ii. You would win at once by the devastating:

2 iii P (promotes)

The whole point is to anticipate this position when you drop your

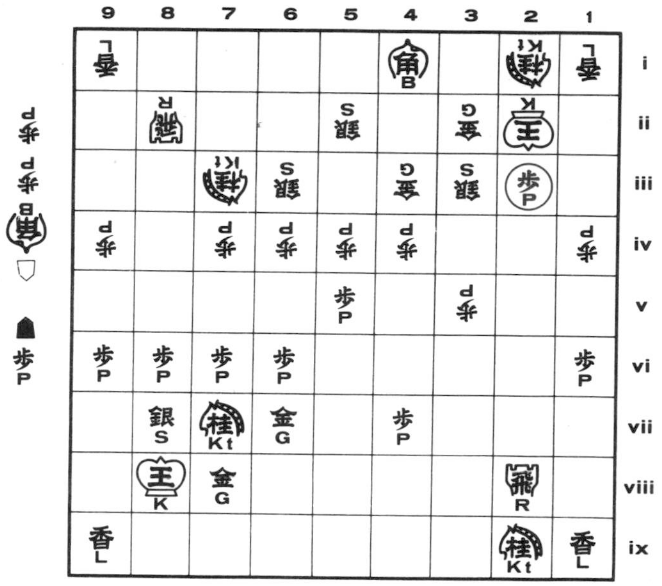

Bishop on 4 i. Of course an expert anticipates it many moves before that.

White's King is directly threatened by the Pawn, which in promoting opens up the lines of the Rook and ultimately those of the Bishop also.

White must now take the Pawn, and he can take it only with his Gold.

This means that he has a Gold on 2 iii, protected by the King, and attacked by both Bishop and Rook. You mate him in two moves (Western chess style, three moves as the Japanese count it, because they count the moves separately instead of in pairs) by playing 2 iii R (promotes) and then Rook or Bishop to 3 ii (mate).

Well, now we assume that White foresees this mating attack and does not take the Silver on 3 v.

Go back now to the diagram on the previous page, and play the following moves, which are the ones given in an analysis by Masuda, one of the foremost experts in Japan today. Note that White's first concern is to knock out all the threatening Bishop drops on the back row.

	. . . 8 i R
2 iii P (promotes)	. . . Same G
2 iv P	. . . 1 iii G

With this move (1 iii G) White brings your attack to a standstill.

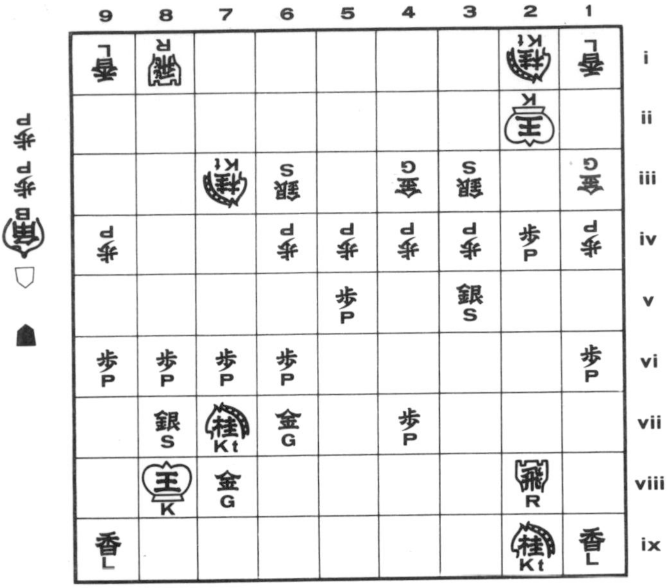

Experiment a bit and see if you can make any progress, and you will find that you cannot.

The point is that a good player is expected to be able to foresee the sequence from the first position given on page 85. In fact Mr. Masuda gave that as one of the questions in a Shogi quiz in a magazine. So it means that as first move, the direct attack by 3 v P, promising though some of the variations look, will end in a deadlock. Therefore you had to find some deeper first move in order to get the right answer to the quiz.

The solution is: (go back to the diagram on page 85)

1 v P

This is a very long-headed move. There is nothing your opponent can do except to take the Pawn. You don't retake but now go on with your original attack. Only at the end, when you get to the standstill position shown in the diagram on this page, will you find that by retaking *now* you can bring new life into the attack. We repeat the moves:

	. . . Same P
3 v P	. . . Same P
Same S	. . . 3 iv P drop
2 iv P	. . . 8 i R
2 iii P (promotes)	. . . Same G
2 iv P drop	. . . 1 iii G
1 v L (diagram)	

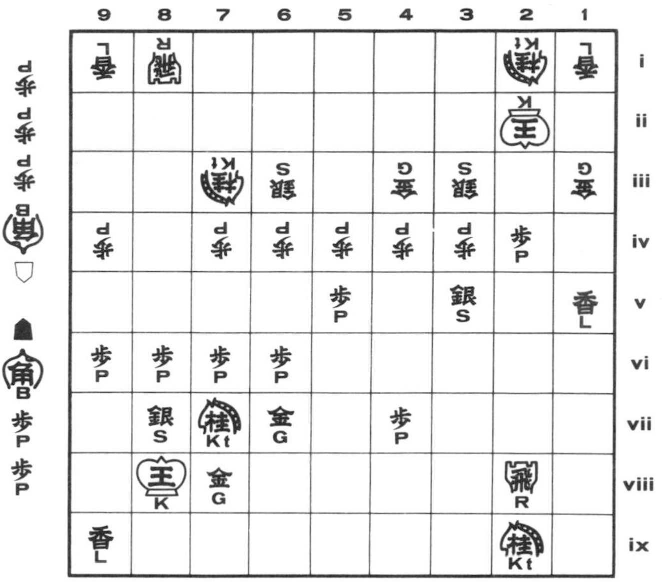

With this move, which was made possible by your sacrifice of the Pawn on 1 v at the beginning, you crumple your opponent's game. If he drops his Pawn on 1 iv, you simply take it with the Lance. He may re-take with his Gold, but in any case you then promote your Pawn on 2 iii.

Your attack, reinforced by the Bishop if necessary, will overwhelm White in a few moves.

After this more or less detailed analysis, you should be able to spot a good many of the possibilities of Shogi combinations. You will be able to follow out the moves in the next positions without too much puzzlement.

Position Two

The diagramed position is from a championship game played in 1949 between Kimura, the challenger and himself a former champion, and Tsukada, the reigning champion. Kimura is Black, this side of the board, and he has just played 2 iv P.

Tsukada resigned, to the surprise of a good many people.

However, if we try over a few variations, it soon becomes clear that White has no chance at all. Suppose for instance that he just goes on with his own attack and plays 4 vii P (promotes). Black answers 2 iii P (promotes), and when White takes this with the Gold, Black drops has Silver on 3 i, forking King and Rook. White has to take it, and Black then promotes his Rook on 2 iii.

☖ 歩 P 歩 P

	9	8	7	6	5	4	3	2	1
i	香 L								香 L
ii		歩 P				飛 R	金 G	王 K	
iii			桂 Kt	銀 S	歩 P		桂 Kt	歩 P	歩 P
iv	歩 P			銀 S			歩 P	歩 P	
v									歩 P
vi	歩 P	銀 S	歩 P	歩 P		歩 P	金 G		
vii		歩 P			歩 P		角 B		
viii		王 K	金 G		金 G		角 B		
ix	香 L	桂 Kt						飛 R	香 L

☗ 銀 S 桂 Kt 歩 P 歩 P

An important point here is that White has only a Silver to drop in defense—a Gold would give him a fighting chance. If he drops on 3 ii, for instance, Black can drop his Gold on 2 ii, exchange off the Silvers, and then settle matters by dropping his Knight on 4 iv.

The main line however is this (from the diagram):

	. . . 2 iv Same P
Same R	. . . 2 iii P drops
3 iv R	. . . 3 v P drops (other moves are equally hopeless)
6 iv R	. . . Same S
3 iv Kt drops	

This Knight fork forces the win quickly. Play over the position a few times to get used to the methods of finishing off the opponent. Notice that in some lines the promoted Bishop on 3 viii can come in forcefully.

Position Three

This also is from a championship match in 1959. Masuda was then champion, and the challenger (White in this game) was the formidable Oyama, many times champion.

Oyama has just achieved the breakthrough with a promoted Rook on 4 ix. Black immediately gets his own Rook through, but White wins this game because his King is comparatively securely defended, with a bodyguard of three, whereas the Black King has only two. White's Knight is not reckoned as one of the defenders because he does not cover any of the squares round the King. Still, he plays a part, because without him Black could try pushing his Pawn to 8 v, and then when it is taken, he could drop a Pawn on 8 iv. In this way he could have tried to keep White busy.

The concluding moves were:

4 iv P drops (to shut out the Bishop)	. . . 1 ix pr. R
2 iii R (promotes)	. . . 8 vii L drops
Same K	. . . 8 ix pr. R
8 viii S	. . . 6 ix B drops
7 ix G drops	. . . 7 viii B (promotes)
Same G	. . . 7 v Kt drops
7 vii K	. . . 7 viii pr. R
Same K	. . . 6 vii G drops
8 ix K	. . . 7 viii G drops
9 viii K	. . . 8 viii G
Same K	. . . 8 vii S drops
9 vii K	. . . 9 v P
7 v P	. . . 7 vii G

Position Four

Only the participating pieces are shown. This is the breakthrough with three Pawns, which must be mastered because it is often the only way to force one's way in. Masters exchange Pawns early in the game mainly to get some in hand for this kind of maneuver.

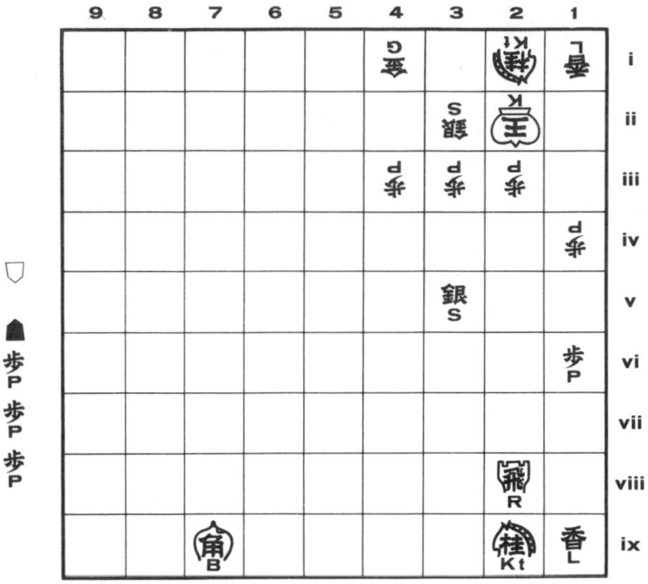

Beginners drop the Pawn on 2 iv, and when White takes, they retake with Silver or Rook. White at once drops his captured Pawn on 2 iii, and Black must retreat. Thus we have the original position, except that Black has wasted his move, for it is now White's turn to play. This is a big tactical defeat for Black.

Correct play is:

2 iv P drops	. . . Same P
2 iii P drops	

The idea is to force the defending Silver forward and knock it out by exchanging. Then the Rook and Bishop from long range, assisted by drops of Silver and Pawns, can force a breakthrough. But there is another pitfall to be avoided:

. . . Same S

A little experiment will show you that White cannot take with the King. 1 v P, threatening to drive him to the edge with a Rook check and then push through with the Lance, would make things too hot for him.

2 iv S	. . . Same S

Position Five

Now comes another crucial move, which beginners always miss even if they got the first one. In the diagramed position they play:

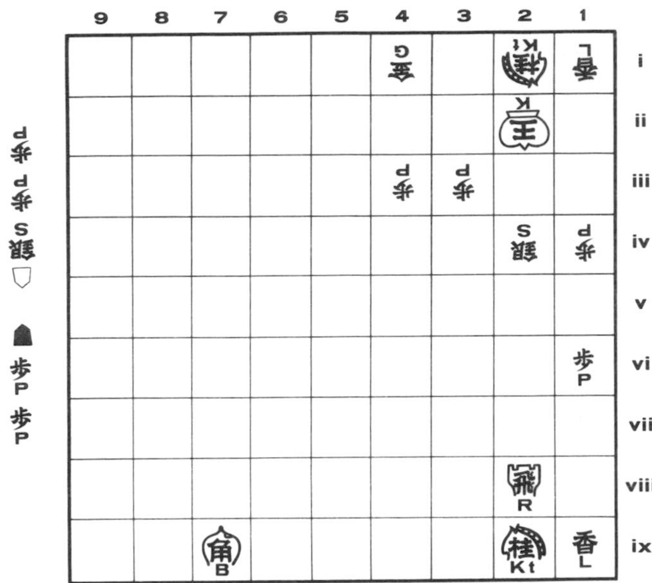

Rook or Bishop takes Silver. White at once drops the Pawn onto 2 iii and things are as they were, except that each side now has a Silver in hand. It is White's move now—a big advantage.

The correct move is the same as before:

2 iii P drops . . . Same K

2 iv B

This is strongest. There are numerous threats. One of them is to promote the Bishop on 1 iii. When the King takes, the Rook shoots down to 2 i, promoting and threatening immediate mate with the captured Knight. The attacks on the edge of the board, opened where necessary by moving the Pawn to 1 v, are always decisive.

Once you get the idea of these Pawn breaks, you'll begin to see them everywhere. Most attacks in Shogi make use of something of the sort. The idea is to *draw the enemy pieces forward;* once advanced, most of the Shogi men cannot so easily get back again, and their formation is irretrievably loosened.

Position Six

Here is a break with only two Pawns. White's defensive formation is defective because the Gold and Silver do not mutually support each other (see page 82). The Gold protects the Silver, but the Silver does not defend the Gold. Stronger would be to have the Gold on 7 i, or to have their positions reversed.

However, it takes skill to turn the weak position of the Gold to your advantage. What you have to do is to force the King away from its defense.

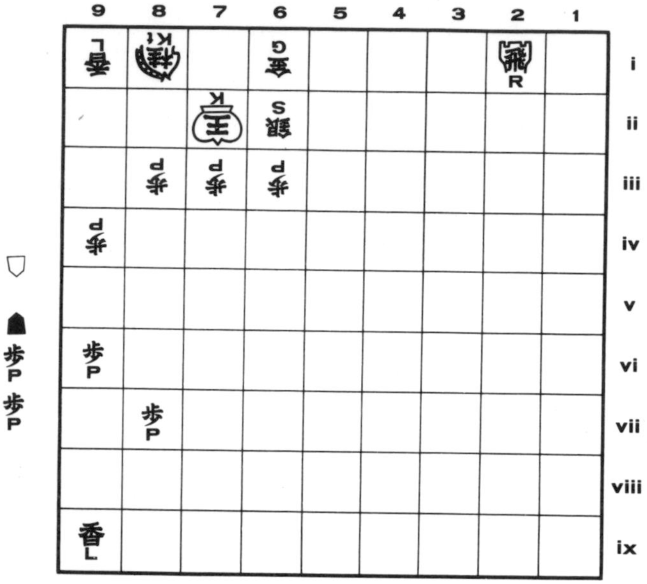

9 v P . . . Same P

9 iii P drops

Now you threaten to take the enemy Pawn with your Lance and push your own Pawn forward to 9 ii, promoting. That would mean the end of White's Lance or Knight, and the collapse of his game.

If he takes the Pawn on 9 iii with the Knight, you do best to drop your last Pawn on 9 ii (try to work out why this is so), then take the Pawn on 9 v. The continuations are similar to the main line.

. . . Same L

9 ii P drops

Next move you promote on 9 i. Whatever he does now—move the King or try to save the Knight—you soon win a piece and the game.

Note: If he took with the Knight as mentioned above, and you went staight ahead taking the Pawn on 9 v, he could have supported his Knight with a Pawn drop himself on 9 ii. You could drive the Knight away and maybe win it, but your breakthrough would be postponed indefinitely.

☗7六歩	☗2五歩	☗同飛	☗2四飛	☗同銀	☗7七角	☗5八金左	☗同玉	☗5三歩
☖3四歩	☖5五歩	☖3二金	☖5六歩	☖3三角	☖8九馬	☖5六飛	☖5八飛成	☖7二玉
☗2六歩	☗2四歩	☗3四飛	☗同歩	☗2一飛成	☗1一角成	☗6八桂	☗同玉	☗5五馬
☖5四歩	☖同歩	☖5二飛	☖8八角成	☖8八角成	☖5七桂	☖4九桂成	☖6二玉	

APPENDIX
How to Read a Japanese Score

Here is the first part of a famous short game played in 1947 between the then-champion, Yoshio Kimura, and the challenger, Masao Tsukada. This is the score just as it looks in a Japanese book or magazine.

Don't get frightened because it looks so unfamiliar; it's quite easy. Remember first that the Japanese write downwards, beginning at the top right corner. So look at the top right, and you'll see the little Black mark and under it the move: 7六歩

That's the first move of the game, and to follow these moves you have first to know that though the top of the board is numbered with the same numerals as ours, the side of the board is numbered not in Roman numbers but with the Japanese numerals.

Here are the Japanese numbers, with the corresponding Roman:

一	i	四	iv	七	vii
二	ii	五	v	八	viii
三	iii	六	vi	九	ix

Not too difficult. The first three obviously are just the same three fingers—but held horizontally instead of vertically. So you only have to learn six new characters.

The first move of Black—7六歩—can be translated as 7 vi P. You remember the character 歩—it comes *in* our representation of the Pawn. To remind you, however, here is the full list again.

Notice that the Japanese give the Rook and Bishop special characters when they are promoted. They give the Pawn one too, and it is と.

When the other pieces are promoted, they keep their original character but have the 成 in front of them.

K	王 K	= 玉			
R	飛 R	= 飛	pr. R	飛 R	= 竜
B	角 B	= 角	pr. B	角 B	= 馬
G	金 G	= 金			
S	銀 S	= 銀	pr. S	銀 S	= 成銀
Kt	桂 Kt	= 桂	pr. Kt	桂 Kt	= 成桂
L	香 L	= 香	pr. L	香 L	= 成香
P	歩 P	= 歩	pr. P	歩 P	= と

The only other characters that come often are these: 同—"Same" So where we write "Same P," the Japanese score will have:

同
歩

The character for promotion is 成. It is used in two ways:

2 iii P (promotes) would appear like this: 2
三
歩
成

You see that 成 comes *after* (i.e. below) the name of the piece that promotes.

Then if a promoted piece is moved, it is written *in front of* the name of the piece. For instance:

8 ii pr. L would be written: 8
二
成
香

Here we go, then, to tackle the first few moves. Try them out on the board, and we shall check with a diagram whether the position is correct.

We shall print the Japanese characters just as they are, and alongside them, the "translation." To help you, we shall number the moves.

No.	☗ (Japanese)	☗ (translation)	☖ (Japanese)	☖ (translation)
①	7六歩	7 vi P	3四歩	3 iv P
②	2六歩	2 vi P	5四歩	5 iv P
③	2五歩	2 v P	5五歩	5 v P
④	2四歩	2 iv P	同歩	Same P
⑤	同飛	Same R	3二金	3 ii G
⑥	3四飛	3 iv R	5二飛	5 ii R
⑦	2四飛	2 iv R	5六歩	5 vi P
⑧	同歩	Same P	8八角成	8 viii B pr.
⑨	同銀	Same S	3三角	3 iii B
⑩	2一飛成	2 i R pr.	8八角成	8 viii B pr.
⑪	7七角	7 vii B	8九馬	8 ix pr. B
⑫	1一角成	1 i B pr.	5七桂	5 vii Kt.
⑬	5八金左	5 viii G (the one on player's left)	5六飛	5 vi R
⑭	6八桂	6 viii Kt.	4九桂成	4 ix Kt. pr.
⑮	同玉	Same K	5八飛成	5 viii R pr.
⑯	同玉	Same K	6二玉	6 ii K
⑰	5三歩	5 iii P	7二玉	7 ii K
⑱	5五馬	5 v pr. B		

(diagrams, see below)

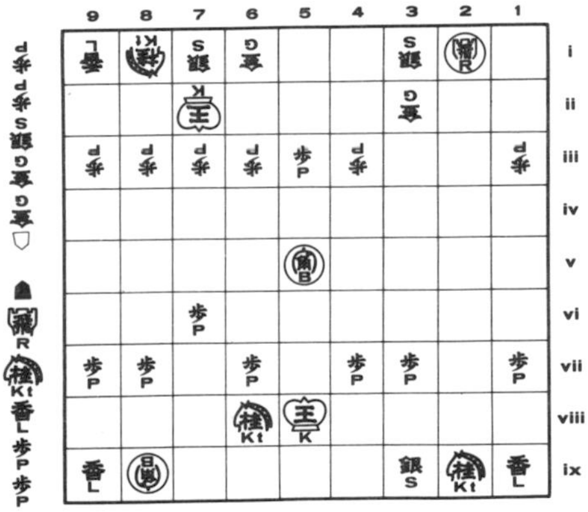

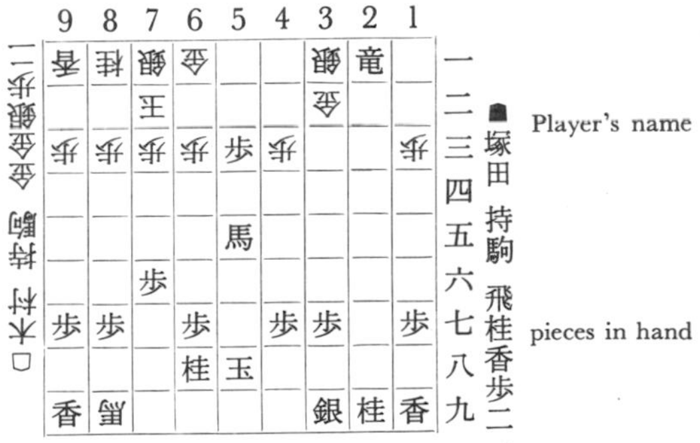

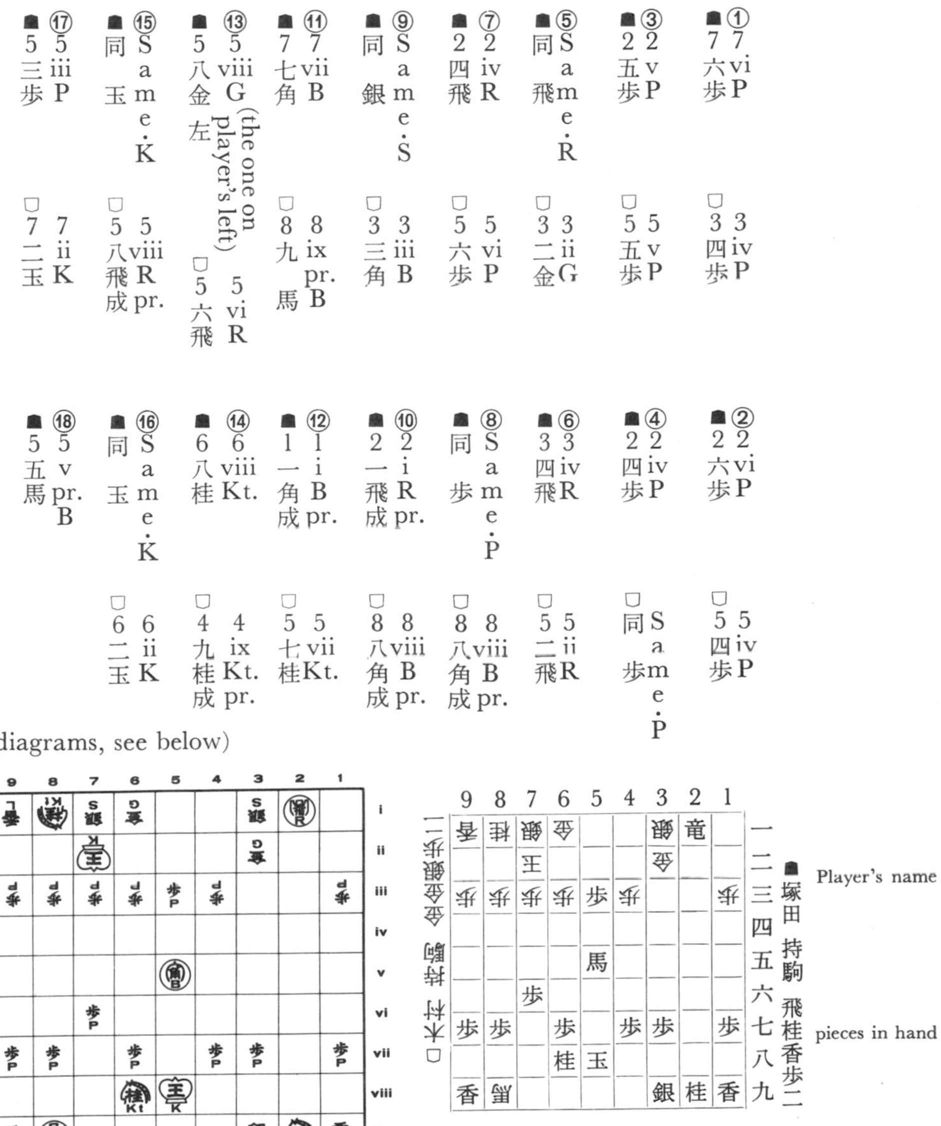

Here are the two diagrams, which you can compare. They represent the same position, and if you have a good look you will soon see how to read the Japanese characters without the little "helps" which we have been giving.

Japanese chess magazines, like *Shogi Sekai* and *Kindai Shogi*, generally give a diagram every ten moves or so, and by referring to them you can check up that your moves have been correct.

Note that in this one Black's pieces in hand have been put on the right—this is a variation sometimes adopted. Also the Pawns are not all put down separately; they have just written 歩 and then 二 (the number for 2) after them. It means each side has two Pawns in hand.

In the score on the previous page there was the unusual case where Black could move either of two identical pieces (in this case Golds) to the same square. The cue is given by writing 左 (left—of the player) or 右 (right—of the player) after the name of the piece.

Similarly, drops are not usually indicated separately; but where an identical piece could move to the same square, the drop is written 打. So 7三歩打 means7 iii P drops.

☖5四歩 ☗同馬 ☖6四金 ☗3六馬
☖5七歩 ☗同玉 ☖8二玉 ☗6六香
☖5九銀 ☗6四香 ☖同歩 ☗7五桂
☖7二銀 ☗6三金 ☖同銀 ☗同馬
☖7二金打 ☗5二歩成 ☖6三金 ☗6一と
☖3五角 ☗4六歩 ☖7九馬 ☗3二竜
☖同銀 ☗8三桂成 ☖同玉 ☗8四銀
まで六十三手 塚田八段の勝

Here is the rest of the game, ending in a win for Tsukada (Black). The last line of the score gives the number of moves and the winner's name. You won't be able to read the name, but by now you know enough Shogi to see which side it is that resigns.

This was a "hell-for-leather" game, in which neither side got the King to safety, but each hoped for a lightning win. This kind of game is most risky and not to be recommended to beginners, but it is put in here because it is short.

As a matter of fact the opening line was regarded as most unfavorable to Black, and it was the move 5 v pr. B (the position shown in the diagram) which surprised White and lost him the game. Even so, the diagram position is quite dangerous for Black also, and it may well be that further resources will be found which will again give the advantage to White. Meanwhile, however, the variation is not being played among the masters.

THERE are a great many foreign visitors who come to know Japan through books, during sight-seeing tours and by personal contacts. However, it is most pleasing to find Mr. Trevor Leggett, the author of the present book on shogi, as one of the very few who are qualified to have a say on something Japanese.

He is the first foreigner to compile a book on the game of shogi. I appreciate his effort and have no hesitation in recommending it to the many shogi enthusiasts all over the world.

Doubtless as one is initiated into a totally new game, one is apt to be puzzled or confused. But when the initial difficulty of learning the name and power of each piece on the board is overcome, the student is bound to be enthralled and derive endless pleasure from the game of shogi.

Interest in the game is now increasing in countries other than Japan, and I am certain that, like judo, there will soon be shogi tournaments held on a world-wide scale.

YASUHARU OYAMA
Shogi Meijin
(Japanese Champion)